and thanks

David Stemp
+ Sophie

A HANDFUL OF BORDER COLLIES

In Memory of Poppi
14/05/2008 to 18/10/2022
A Border Collie with Attitude

First Published in Great Britain in April 2024
by David Stemp, 27, Netley Close, Cheam, Surrey SM3 8DN
Telephone - 0208 641 5765
Email - david.stemp@virgin.net
Copyright © 2024 David Stemp
ISBN: 978-0-9525910-8-5
Printed in Great Britain
by SW19 Design & Print, Wimbletech, Marlborough Hall,
Compton Road, Wimbledon SW19 7QA
Telephone - 0800 599 9597
Email - design@sw19designandprint.co.uk
Website - www.sw19designandprint.co.uk

Introduction

The eponymous character in 'The Love Song of J. Alfred Prufrock' by T.S. Eliot declared in a rather melancholy fashion that *"I have measured out my life with coffee spoons"*. In comparison to J. Alfred Prufrock the last forty two years of my life have been measured out by five wonderful, interesting and entertaining Border Collies, who have allowed me to share their lives.

For forty two years, therefore, my life has revolved around my Border Collies who have accompanied me almost everywhere. I have been fortunate enough to own five dogs who loved spending hours on end with me, often cooped up in a car. Apart from travelling around Surrey and the Home Counties watching me play cricket for Worcester Park and Surrey Seniors, they were regular visitors at Cuddington Golf Course, where at least they had a decent walk.

On four occasions some of my furry friends even travelled as far as the French Alps, which at the speed that I drive usually meant that they spent at least seven hours per day in the car for three or four consecutive days, as I usually took the scenic route around France avoiding large cities and motorways. I learnt at an early stage that to entrust the dogs to kennels was often a recipe for disaster in the form of kennel cough or upset tummies.

There are so many memories and photographs of Ben, Benji, Gemma, Poppi and finally Sophie that, after the death of Poppi, a dog whom I eventually grew to love after a very rocky start, I decided to write a short book, which to a great extent is an autobiography based around these marvellous dogs, detailing some of their adventures, in the hope that perhaps it might inspire more dog lovers to adopt a Border Collie.

I must apologise to the reader for the quality of the photographs of Ben, Benji and Gemma as like my memories, they seem to have faded slightly. It could be, however, that my modern Android phone is just better than still shots taken from my video camera or my old Box Brownie. That explains the photographs, as to the faded memories, I think that old age could be responsible.

Hopefully anyone who does read this book might also pick up a few tips upon how to treat these intelligent dogs and to learn perhaps from my mistakes. Remember, however, that no two Border Collies are alike. Some can be highly strung whilst others are laid back. Each has its own personality and interesting traits. If you show them love and respect they will be faithful and loyal until the end, which sadly comes too soon. That is the real downside of becoming attached to any animal.

****

The first thirty seven years of my life were basically Collie-less and as a result can be skimmed over. One of the most interesting facts of that life, however, was that I was conceived in Stornoway on the Isle of Lewis in the Outer Hebrides, when my mother, née Bessie Peters, visited her husband Harold Stanley Stemp who was stationed there as a corporal barber in the R.A.F. Coastal Command, where he was billeted with a few of his fellow comrades at the home of a Mrs. Fraser.

Being a barber in the R.A.F. sounds like a cushy non-operational role, but it was fraught with danger from enemy bombing, as my father had found out to his cost three years earlier when he was stationed at Pembroke Docks. Following a night-time German attack he was hospitalised at R.A.F. Haverfordwest for several months. Stornoway was, however, a slightly less dangerous hair-dressing location.

Because my father had managed to pull a few strings in 1944, Bessie was booked in as a passenger on the inaugural flight of what was to become a thrice weekly Scottish Airways Service from Inverness to Stornoway on Saturday May 26th. The plane was a frail looking bi-plane, a D. H. Rapide, which held less than a dozen passengers, amongst whom were the Lord Provost of Inverness, the Provost of Glasgow, the Town Clerk of Stornoway and a couple of other high ranking dignitaries.

Although the side windows of the plane were blacked out for security reasons, the passengers did notice through the windows next to the pilot that there seemed to be hundreds of small ships below in the Minch sailing southwards. Bessie discovered shortly thereafter that these ships had been part of the preparations for D Day.

Nine months later at 3.20 p.m. on February 28th, and weighing 7lbs. 4ozs., I was born at Queens Park Hospital in Blackburn. As this was before the NHS, we were allowed to stay in the hospital until March 12th before we returned to Bessie's childhood home at 62, Hollins Grove, Street, Darwen, where she lived with her widowed father, seventy years old Bill Peters. It was another month before my father managed to meet me as he was still stationed at Stornoway. I think that I probably bonded more with my mother in that first year rather than with the leather clad stranger on a motorcycle.

It was not until the end of my first year that my father was demobbed. As a corporal barber in the R.A.F. for six years he had managed to save enough from his pay, and from the tips that he received from his customers, to buy a hairdressing business outright. On February 11th, 1946, he signed a contract with Maurice Rogers, a hairdresser of 96, Barkerhouse Road, Nelson, to buy his shop, the house and all the utensils and stock for the grand sum of £315.

Shortly after that, with the house in Darwen having been sold, the small family, plus Bill Peters and most of his furniture, moved into the tiny terraced property in Nelson,

Three months later Harold must have realised that a motorcycle and a young family were not really compatible, as on May 10th, 1946, he bought a second hand sandy coloured Austin 7 in exchange for his Matchless Motorcycle and £90.

Most of the first nineteen years of my life, therefore, was spent in a row of terraced houses that had been built in the late Victorian era from blocks of millstone grit, which had become blackened by years of industrial pollution from the nearby cotton mills.

The rubric on the shop window of 96, Barkerhouse Road, rather grandiosely stated that it was a hairdressing salon and tobacconists which also sold toiletries. Basically it was one tiny room with a couple of hairdressing chairs and a padded bench upon which waiting customers sat. The display in the window seemed to be made up of jars of Brylcreem with the compulsory picture of Dennis Compton, bars of Knights Castile, boxes of cigars and ornate tobacco pipes.

Beside the shop was a small corridor which led from the front door to the living room, which was extremely crowded with furniture as it was the only communal living space in the house. The focus of the room was the black metal fireplace which provided the only source of heating, and above which hung a large wooden clothes rack suspended by ropes and pulleys. It was before this fire that I used to bathe in a large corrugated tin bathtub every Friday night.

Passing through the sitting room one came to the kitchen, which contained the cooker and the Bendix washing machine which seemed to flood almost every week. The window in the kitchen overlooked the backyard which contained the outside toilet and the coal shed. I have a very faint memory of seeing my father's motorbike there which he disposed of when I was fifteen months old. It is strange that it is sometimes easier to remember events from the distant past rather than what one did an hour ago.

It was not an ideal place to own a dog, but in late 1948 my parents bought our first family dog which has led to me being a dog lover or cynophile for almost 76 years.

That tiny bundle of joy who entered my life was Patsy Fagin, aka Pat, a small rough haired, sandy coloured terrier, who was born on the 24th February, 1947. I was only three years old when we acquired him the following year and, as I had no siblings at that stage, until the birth of my brother Bill in 1949, we became very close. He was my earliest friend and companion and we had many real and imaginary adventures together. On the right is a rather grainy picture of him sitting up and begging for a biscuit from my mother.

Probably the most memorable scrape that Pat and I got into together was in the summer of 1948 when we crashed the family's Austin Seven into a large stone wall. It was one Sunday morning and for some unknown reason my father had left Pat and his three year old son in the car unattended on the steep cobbled back street. Social Services would probably have become involved nowadays but in those days…..

I had been pretending to drive the car and accidentally released the handbrake. The car slowly moved backwards down the slope, crossed Fir Street and gathering pace crashed into the stone wall of Mrs. Pengelly's house in Roberts Street. I remember vividly jumping from the front seat to the back seat and back again before the impact.

The accident attracted quite an audience. Fortunately neither the driver nor his four legged accomplice were injured. Mrs. Pengelly's wall was unmarked, which sadly was not the fate of the back of the tiny Austin Seven which was severely dented, and meant that my rather angry father had to spend the rest of the day trying to repair it.

Strangely enough I can vividly remember another couple of incidents involving that tiny car. On one occasions when I was just two years old, in the Winter of 1947, my father had to dig the car out of a snow drift as he attempted to get over the tops to Darwen, whilst on another occasion we had a minor bump with a car full of medical students whilst driving through Manchester.

I think that my mother must have been responsible for the family acquiring Pat as she was definitely an animal lover. My father, on the other hand, usually gave the impression that he did not like dogs, although secretly I think that he did. Coming from an agricultural family, he had been brought up with dogs and tended to see them more as functional rather than as pets. He was the one, however, who ended up walking the dog every evening.

Life was not easy for that little dog as my father was a hard task master and insisted that Pat slept in a kennel in the backyard, near the coal shed and the outside lavvie. If, however, the gate to the backyard was left open by a neighbour or sometimes by myself, Pat would disappear. I can remember the despair that I felt on several occasions as I wandered the streets calling his name, wondering if I would ever see the little man again. Sometimes he disappeared for three or four days at a time before either returning of his own accord or being brought back by one of my father's customers.

Pat was so gentle with my brother and myself, although we must often have made his life a misery as we dressed him up to take part in a variety of imaginary games in our special den beneath the dining room table. Probably the best example of Pat's lovely nature was the fact that we had a budgerigar called Peter who, if he saw Pat sitting on the armchair, used to fly on to the back of the chair and slowly walk down the arm before proceeding to nibble the poor dog's ear, forcing him to leave his seat and take shelter under the sideboard. Pat would never have thought of turning upon the budgie or any member of the family.

Another great example of Pat's lovely temperament can be seen from the fact that one morning, he was extremely reluctant to come out of his kennel. Eventually my father dragged him out and discovered that a dead rat was hidden in the straw bedding. The poor little dog obviously thought that he would be punished for killing the rat, rather than being praised for destroying vermin.

Pat was the ideal companion for two young children who used to drag him everywhere. The photograph on the right shows Pat and myself in 1949 digging in the sand at Southport.

One of my most unforgettable memories of Pat occurred on a family holiday to Littlehampton in about 1951. Somehow he had managed to end up on a sandbank in a tidal river which entered the sea. The canalised banks of the river looked, to a small child, to be about ten feet tall, and the tide was coming in. Pat's life was in jeopardy until one brave young man amongst the crowd of onlookers, with the help of his friends, managed to scramble down and pass the little dog to safety.

Pat's death on July 26th 1960 came as a shock to my brother Bill and myself, although my parents tried to cushion the blow by taking us out for a treat. It was a Tuesday afternoon, a half day for shopkeepers, and my father decided to take Bill and myself to Bolton Abbey. My mother stayed at home with Pat to await the arrival of the vet. By the time we returned our lovely little friend was dead.

We felt that no other dog could replace Pat until a couple of years later we acquired a small mongrel puppy with wonky ears, which we called Midge as she was the smallest in the litter. Not for her a cold kennel in a wet backyard. She was immediately welcomed into the house and the family.

Although I was a member of the family group for the first couple of years of the puppy's life, after September 1964 my contact with Midge was severely curtailed when I left home to study at the College of St. Mark and St. John in Chelsea. I usually only returned home for a few days at Christmas, Easter or during the summer holidays. As I spent most of these holidays catching up with old friends I am afraid that I did not spend as much time with Midge as perhaps I would have liked.

My brother Bill spent a lot more time with Midge than I did. His most abiding

memory of that sweet dog is of the day that he and June, his wife-to-be, took her to Victoria Park in Nelson. Midge made a bee-line for the ornamental lake, jumped in and proceeded to chase the swans. As the dog refused to return Bill's only option was to wade knee deep into the lake to retrieve her.

The longest time I spent with Midge was when I took her camping in the Lake

District for a few days in my small black A30, with Colin Shanley one of my friends from Nelson Grammar School. Midge and Colin were sharing breakfast in the photograph on the previous page. Midge probably enjoyed the short holiday more than I did, as, if I remember rightly, it was quite a damp experience.

Midge tended to accompany my parents wherever they went on holiday around the British Isles. The photograph on the left, which was taken in around 1965, however, shows my parents and Midge standing outside the backyard of our house next to my black A30.

One can see the blackened millstone grit blocks in the wall behind them and the steep cobbled back street down which I had driven their Austin Seven about twenty years before. My father still operated as a hairdresser from the front room of the house, which by this stage had acquired an inside toilet and the coal shed was no longer needed.

My mother was the driving force behind the family. As a teenager she had attended Darwen Grammar School but had to leave school at sixteen to help her aged parents financially. She studied hard at night school and acquired certificates in commerce, shorthand and secretarial skills and worked for the local council.

Following her marriage to Harold Stemp, the move to Nelson and the birth of myself, her first job was in Mr. Miller's chip shop in Larch Street, three or four nights a week. Although she enjoyed the experience as she loved the social interaction, it did not really make use of her secretarial skills. A year or two later she was offered, and accepted, a job managing the radio shop next door at 94, Barkerhouse Road, which was taken over shortly thereafter by Rediffusion. That company quickly realised her potential and offered her the job of Office Manageress for the Nelson and Burnley area overseeing an office staff of ten.

In 1965, she took on another challenge when she accepted the role of Secretary of the Association of Teachers of Mathematics which existed in a small office in a back street in Nelson, from where she was responsible for producing their regular Mathematic journal, which was distributed not only in the U.K. but throughout the world. She was also responsible for organizing, and attended, conferences for Mathematic teachers at universities, not only in the U.K. but occasionally at venues such as the University of California, Berkeley.

My mother was also heavily involved in our local church where she was the Secretary of the Parochial Church Council, and at a later date became the Secretary of the Diocesan Council. In her spare time, which was extremely limited, she was a member of the Colne and District Writers' Circle, where she wrote this moving tribute to Midge following her death in 1977.

Midge

Dear Midge you came to live with us,
So very long ago.
A tiny, trembling, furry thing
Afraid and full of woe.
I took you gently in my arms,
And murmured in your ear,
Your trembling ceased, you gave
your trust,
And we dispelled your fear.

Your coat grew soft and shone like silk,
Your tail waved as you trod,
But you weren't entirely handsome,
For your ears were really odd.
You gave us all your loyalty,
Whilst to you we gave the same.
Oh how you loved to romp and play
And join the children's game.

You couldn't pass a puddle,
You were like a little child;
You'd splash in any water,
Be the weather cold or mild.
You were seldom ever left alone,
But whenever so saw red,
You'd scurry up the stairs
And upset all the bed.

Now fifteen years have quickly passed,
We dearly loved you so,
Though you were getting very old
We didn't want to know,
Until you fell and screamed in pain,
I nursed you little friend.
Your body eased, your trust returned,
But we knew this was the end.

In 1966 my love of dogs led me to briefly acquire Bobby, an eleven week old puppy, whom I came across whilst I was on a geography field trip to Swansea with Marjons. Whilst supposedly drawing sketch maps of the topography of the Gower Peninsula, I came across a farmer in Bishopston whose bitch had recently had a litter of puppies. I was attracted by one of the puppies and agreed to return to the farm on the day of our departure to collect him.

The following Saturday morning I picked up the little dog, put him in a duffle bag, got on the coach and took him back to Chelsea. I then drove down to my grandmother's home in Cranleigh and presented her with, what I thought was a lovely present as she had recently lost her husband. Unfortunately she failed to agree, but he was welcomed into the home of her nephew Ken Doyle, his wife Nancy and daughter Leslie. The picture on the  right shows Bobby standing, rejected outside my grandmother's gate.

After college I spent five years in a small flat in Sutton before climbing onto the housing ladder with a two bedroom terraced property in Brandy Way, South Sutton, which was not really ideal for dog ownership. It was, however, while tutoring Anita Owen, a privately educated young lady at Greenacres, that I first encountered Border Collies. Her family lived in a large house in South Sutton with stables at the bottom of the garden. When I first met Anita she had a beautiful Collie bitch called Lady. Sadly Lady died after being kicked by one of the horses, and was replaced by Laddie, who seemed an equally friendly dog.

On a couple of occasions I was asked to stay in the house for a week to look after Laddie. It was quite a terrifying experience. The house was an imitation Dutch Barn that creaked all night long as the wood expanded and contracted. It sounded as though someone was walking around. I jammed the bedroom door shut and slept with an extremely sharp Japanese Samurai sword, which had been surrendered to Anita's father in 1945, beside my bed.

I also discovered that Laddie was far from friendly if one approached him whilst he was eating. From being an extremely lovely dog whom one could stroke and pet, as soon as his dish hit the floor he became a snarling canine psychopath. I must admit that experience gave me a rather negative feeling for the breed.

On August 21st, 1981, I sold my small property in Brandy Way and moved into a four bed-roomed, three storey town house overlooking Cheam Rec. and Nonsuch Park. Although the house only had a tiny garden at the rear, which could be accessed via a small side gate, at the front lay the 62 acres of Cheam Park and the Recreation ground, whilst at the western edge of the Park, beyond a narrow wooded area, lay the 250 acres of Nonsuch Park, a Mecca for dog owners for miles around.

The photograph on the right was taken in about 1995, by which time a small porch had been added to the front of the house and a conservatory to the rear.

Unfortunately the move came at a price as I had to sell both my old Voltswagen Beetle and my lovely, S registered M.G. Midget, which I had bought in the West End.

I have had about 25 different cars but that Midget, which I had bought from new was easily my favourite, although it was probably not ideal for a dog owner, but for an eligible young bachelor dashing around the countryside with the wind rushing through his hair, it was the perfect car.

The photograph on the left which was taken by my father, shows me sitting on the bonnet of the M.G. displaying a tie and trophy which I had won in a Pool competition at Sutton Tennis and Squash Club in about 1980.

By that stage I had become enamoured by a small Yorkshire Terrier called Barnie, that belonged to a former girlfriend, Ann. I became determined to take the plunge and buy a Yorkshire Terrier the following spring. Little did I know that the Yorkie would grow into a 20 Kilogram long haired Border Collie called Ben.

****

Ben - A Collie Nonpareil

An Impulse Buy

As Thursday April 15th 1982 was in the Easter holidays I took the opportunity to cycle into Sutton that afternoon, not really expecting to buy a dog but to browse. My destination was Petsville a rather dubious and odorous pet shop at the bottom of Sutton High Street which was often the focus of protesters campaigning against puppy farming and the conditions in which the animals were kept.

There were no protestors or Yorkies that day but in a cage at the back of the shop was one solitary, sad looking, tiny nine week old Border Collie in a rather dirty cage, who had obviously only recently been separated from his mother. Any of his siblings who had travelled with him from Wales to Sutton had already found new homes. Why had he not been chosen? Was he the runt of the litter? These and many more questions coursed through my head.

For me it was love at first sight. I wanted to rescue that little fellow who sat there extremely quietly with his ears flattened. He had almost classical Collie markings of four white paws, a white tip to the tail, a white undercarriage, a white collar and a slightly off-centre white stripe down the centre of his face. The photograph on the left shows him, still looking slightly despondent at about seven or eight months old.

The invoice gave his date of birth as February 10th, and his place of origin as being Cottage Kennels, Cardigan. It also claimed that he was black and white when, as can be seen from the adjoining photograph, he was obviously tricolour as there were traces of brown around his eyes and on his legs. With V.A.T. he cost the grand sum of £40.25, plus £11.90 for his vaccination. It was the best £52.15 that I have ever spent, and I could even afford to buy a Dog Licence for 37½p.

Being a hoarder I still have that Licence; a faded photograph of which can be seen on the opposite page. For a legal document it left a lot to be desired. It is about four by six inches in size (14 x 11 cms) and is printed upon extremely poor quality paper which is reminiscent of Izal Medicated Toilet Tissue. On the front side, however, was a stark warning that the *'Penalty for refusing to show this Licence to any duly authorised officer, or Police Constable, or for keeping a dog above six months old without Licence, £10.'*

On the rear of the Licence there was information about Road Safety, the Worrying of Sheep, Cattle and Poultry, Rabies and Dog Collars which people probably rarely read but which contained some useful information such as how to spot a rabid dog and what to do next. It also stated that it was a crime to *'allow your dog to be on a highway or in a public place without a collar bearing your name and address.'*

The dog licence was an anachronism which had been introduced in 1867 for the price of 7 shillings and 6 pence. Using the Bank of England inflation calculator that was equivalent to £35. When I bought a licence for Ben 115 years later in 1982, the price was still the same in decimal currency - 37½ pence. It is interesting to note that two years later, when the halfpenny was scrapped as currency, the licence was reduced in price to 37 pence.

In 1988, however, as less than half of dog owners could be bothered to buy a dog licence, the scheme was eventually scrapped in England, Wales and Scotland, although dog licences are still necessary in Northern Ireland.

Journey Home - After about half an hour I left the store with the invoice and the vaccination certificate tucked into my back pocket, struggling to carry one large cardboard box which contained the puppy, a shiny silver coloured metal dish, a plastic water bowl, a collar and lead and enough dog food to last several days.

The fact that I had cycled into Sutton shows that I had obviously not really expected to buy a dog that day. It was impossible to cycle and hold the box. This meant that I had to balance the box on the handle bars and push the bike the two miles to Netley Close. It was difficult and tiring and rather worrying as I could feel the little puppy beginning to move around.

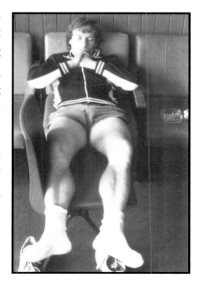

Fortunately my route took me along Collingwood Road past the house of one of my colleagues at Glastonbury High School, Bob Ormsby the P.E. teacher, who owed me a favour or two as I had fed the poor ever-hungry, newly qualified teacher at my previous address. This rather undignified photograph on the right shows Bob relaxing in the staff room between lessons.

The school was a small Surrey bi-lateral school on the St. Helier Estate with a grammar stream and a C.S.E. stream. Because it was small, one knew every pupil and often their family. Although the sport facilities were extremely poor by today's standards, we turned out some exceptional football, cricket, tennis and badminton teams, thanks to the hundreds of hours of unpaid overtime which were devoted to the pupils after school and at weekends. No wonder Bob could sometimes be found taking a short nap in the staff room.

When we arrived at his house Bob was not there but Jenny, his wife, was quite happy to look after the little dog until Bob and his car returned home. It was a couple of hours later that Ben and I became re-united, but it had given me time to line the kitchen floor with plastic sheets and newspapers, a condition that remained in place for at least six weeks whilst Ben became house trained.

TIP NUMBER 1 - it is best that one either obtains a dog from a Rescue or from a recognised breeder, as one is liable to inherit a host of possible medical problems if a puppy's ancestry is shrouded in mystery.

Unfortunately I did not follow that advice and within 24 hours Ben and I found ourselves in the waiting room of Dodds and Phillips, Veterinarians of Mulgrave Road, South Sutton. The poor tiny dog had a touch of colitis and sickness, a problem which beset him throughout his life.

Among the many and varied problems which occurred on his medical record was epilepsy which required EEG tests (1984), lipoma (1986), blocked tear ducts (1991), respiratory problems (1992), alopecia (1993), hypothyroid (1993), prostate gland (1994), arthritis (1997), tumours (1997), and anal adenoma (1997).

It is ironic that despite all those problems from which he suffered throughout his life he survived longer than any of his successors and stayed alert until the very end.

House Training Ben

I will not pretend that it was easy to house train Ben, as the kitchen, dining room and sitting room are all on the first floor of the three storey townhouse. Ben was kept mainly in the kitchen, the floor of which was copiously covered in old newspapers. He was regularly taken down to the garden where he was praised whenever he did a wee or poo. After about a six weeks he would whine if ever he wanted to go out.

For his successors, however, house training was much easier as in 1993 a conservatory was built at the rear of the house, the door of which could be left ajar. The situation improved even further in 2000 when a dog flap and radiators were added, making the conservatory into a very expensive and luxurious canine kennel,

TIP NUMBER 2 - it is advisable to let a young dog out immediately after it has eaten, as taking in sustenance at one end tends to trigger an autonomic response at the other end.

Ben the House Dog

Once Ben was house trained he had full run of the property. As it was a large townhouse there were two flights of stairs. His favourite resting spot was either behind the full length window in the lounge where he could watch any passers-by in the park, or he would lie on the second step down on the top flight of the stairs where the steps changed direction, This was a slightly larger step and from there he could  watch anyone entering or leaving six different rooms on the top two floors. At night time, although he had a small bed on the floor of the kitchen, in his latter years he tended to sleep outside his master's room on the top floor.

Educating Ben

Ben had a great understanding of the spoken word and was the easiest of my dogs to train to obey simple commands such as 'sit' and 'stay'. I was not really interested in having him do tricks, I merely wanted him to be a friendly house dog. Having been both an English teacher and a Special Needs teacher for over thirty years, I merely employed the same technique of constant repetition and praise to train him.

When Ben was 12 weeks old and had had all his injections, we walked the 120 yards to the entrance of the park. I was a little nervous and kept him on an extendable lead to begin with, although he already seemed to be quite attached to me and did not appear to be inclined to leave my side.

A few days later I decided that I would risk letting him off the lead. As an added precaution, however, I did make sure that the park gate was closed. We walked about 300 yards up the slope before I removed the lead. There was no real reaction so I tried running down the hill, and was pleased to note that he immediately chased after me as fast as his little legs could move. It was probably the only time I beat him at running until he was thirteen when I tried to race him again. That was a decision that I came to regret as he pulled up lame and was never quite as mobile for the rest of his life.

TIP NUMBER 3 - be aware of the physical limitations of the Border Collie as over-doing an activity can lead to injury. Limit the time spent on any activity.

Sadly I learnt at an early stage that a Border Collie was often oblivious to pain and danger. Whilst Ben was still very young I had to look after a friend's house with a circular swimming pool. Whilst swimming lengths of the pool one afternoon Ben ran round and round the pool barking. I thought that it was quite amusing. It was not until

I noticed blood on the concrete that I realised that he had taken the skin off all four paws. Again an expensive visit to the vet ensued.

If ever I spotted Ben doing an activity such as rolling over, shaking or stretching I would say the appropriate word or phrase such as "Roll Over", "Shake" or "Stretch" so that he associated the action with the word. The "Shake" command is particularly useful if the dog is wet through, although it is probably best not to stand too close. This photograph is a good example of a stretch.

I rarely used treats to train him, apart from Choc Drops for Dogs, to which he was extremely partial. The one area of his behaviour where I failed miserably was to stop him pulling on the lead, although this behaviour ceased after eighteen months. As a result I automatically expected Ben's successors, Benji and Gemma, to also stop pulling at around the same age. I was sadly wrong as they continued pulling for several years.

TIP NUMBER 4 - Do NOT give dogs chocolate as it can be fatal.

One of the most embarrassing episodes which happened when Ben was a puppy occurred one beautiful warm afternoon, whilst we were walking across Nonsuch Park. Ben saw a scantily dressed sunworshipper lying flat out on the grass. He charged over and jumped on the man's naked chest. It must have been a terrifying experience for the poor bloke. Both hands suddenly thrust upwards, throwing the equally surprised puppy at least four feet into the air. I kept a closer eye on him after that.

Border Collies are exceptionally clever as is shown by the work of a retired American psychologist, John Pilley who taught his Border Collie, Chaser, to understand over 1,100 words. Ben undoubtedly understood several hundred words as I constantly talked to him and pointed out objects of interest around the house or in the park.

At one stage in his book, as an example of Chaser's intelligence, John Pilley claimed that his dog had invented a game whereby Chaser would drop a ball down the stairs and expected John to throw it back to him. I'm afraid that the joys of throwing a ball downstairs and watching it bounce from step to step is a game that has been played by all my Collies. If I did not throw it back they would race downstairs, pick up the ball, dash back to the top of the stairs and repeat the operation. Was this really a sign of exceptional intelligence? If so, all my Border Collies were very intelligent.

One or two words really seemed to pique Ben's attention and his ears would stand on end. His apparent interest in one word baffled me. As part of my Special Needs' work in 1988 I had to visit a Special School in Angmering. Ben accompanied me on that trip and spent several hours asleep in the car. I noticed after that trip that whenever I mentioned the word 'Angmering' to anyone, Ben's ears would immediately shoot up and his head would rock to one side. Why? I have no idea!

Ben and Glastonbury High School

For the first five years of Ben's life I taught at Glastonbury High School, Morden, which was about a couple of miles away from Netley Close. It meant that, on the whole, I had no problem looking after a dog as the school was only a ten minutes' drive away from home, if all the stars were aligned.

During term time we fell into quite a regular routine. We would go into the park at about 7 a.m., chase a ball on a rope before returning home for breakfast. It was on one of these first early morning runs that we met Colin, a rather large, blunt B.T. engineer and his Springer Spaniel Sally. Whilst the dogs chased the ball or each other, Colin and I would put the world to rights. He was one of those individuals who had a dogmatic opinion upon every topic under the sun. On one occasion when the park was not opened on time he even produced a set of wire cutters to gain access. Sadly Sally died a couple of years later from Weil's Disease which she had picked up in one of the stagnant ponds in Nonsuch Park.

TIP NUMBER 5 - it is advisable that a dog does not eat for at least an hour before undergoing strenuous activity as it can lead to stomach problems.

TIP NUMBER 6 - ponds and stagnant water can also be extremely dangerous.

Following breakfast I would then drive to school before returning home at lunchtime for a sandwich and another short walk. Occasionally if I had a free period before lunch I bunked off even earlier. If I knew that I would be unable to return at lunchtime, however, Ben usually travelled into school with me and stayed in the car under the shade of the trees, with the windows and sunroof slightly ajar.

On a few occasions he even attended my sixth form Literature lessons, although Chaucer seemed to be beyond his comprehension.

The photograph on the right shows us standing besides the tennis courts on Sutton Common Rec. where we were helping to supervise a game's lesson.

Ben and Other Dogs

I rarely put Ben on the lead in the park in those early days as he seldom wandered any distance away from me and would come whenever I whistled. As he became older, however, problems began to arise if ever a large male dog came near me. He would square up to the other dog and more often than not a fight would ensue. On more than one occasion I found myself on my knees, with my hands tightly clenched around the collar of each dog, straining to keep them apart. More by luck than management I survived without being bitten, but it made me very wary of coming into close contact with most other dog walkers, unless I knew the sex of the dog.

Ben never went looking for trouble but could handle himself in a fight. He would immediately go for the neck and throw the other dog down. I only saw him on the losing side once when he squared up to a Rhodesian Ridgeback that grabbed him by the scruff of the neck and shook him about. Ben's medical records, however, show that he did not always escape unscathed as I was billed in November, 1987 for stitches that he had received as the result of a dog fight.

Ben became much more amenable after he was castrated at the age of about twelve to help with his prostate condition. It is a shame that I flinched from making that decision many years earlier.

TIP NUMBER 7 - it is probably best to have your dog neutered if you wish to make friends with other dog owners and avoid unnecessary vet bills.

Ben and Work post Glastonbury H.S.

Life became rather more difficult in 1987 when Glastonbury High School, a school that I loved, was closed by the local education authority as a result of falling numbers. Although I really wanted to take very early retirement so that I could spend more time playing cricket and golf, the borough kept finding me new jobs. I spent a year as Head of History at Highview H.S. and then another at Greenshaw H.S. studying Special Needs.

This was followed by a further twelve years in the Special Needs Department at Stanley Park H.S. in Carshalton where I was responsible for creating an extremely successful paired reading scheme which featured in an episode of 'Your Shout' on I.T.V. in December 1994.

The move to Highview H.S. and Stanley Park H.S. made dog ownership a little more difficult as they were both over four miles away and most of the lunch hour was taken up driving between Carshalton and Cheam, sometimes at slightly excessive speeds. I was twice pulled up by the police. On the first occasion a police officer jumped into the road with his hand in the air and asked me how fast I was going. Fortunately I remained calm and said '30 miles per hour'. As he had no proof to the contrary I was sent on my way with a warning. On the second occasion a police car pulled me over very close to the school just as pupils were returning from lunch. I explained that I was late for registration. The driver, seeing the sniggering passers-by, just warned me to be more careful in future.

On some occasions, when the weather as not too warm, I had to keep Ben in the car all day. I would park in the shade, leave the windows ajar, and endeavour to walk him in the morning break and at lunchtime in a local park. Thankfully all my Border Collies have loved being in a car. The problem has often been to stop them getting in the car when my back has been turned as that could be dangerous.

Ben had suffered from car-sickness when he was a puppy but by the time I moved to Stanley Park he had totally outgrown it.

TIP NUMBER 8 - it is probably best to feed your dog at least an hour and a half before a long car journey to lessen the chance of sickness.

Ben the Cricket Mascot

By the time he was three months old Ben attended his first cricket match, a Worcester Park Third XI game at Gibraltar Rec. in Ewell. He soon became very popular with the younger players, who would play with him before the match and during the tea interval. I actually came to regret allowing him this freedom as, on May 30th, an incidence occurred which I can vividly see in my mind's eye even today. Whilst some of the lads were knocking up before the game, fourteen year old Steven Vickery straight drove a ball into the centre of Ben's forehead as the dog chased towards him. Ben fell to the ground stunned. He quickly recovered and I thought nothing more about it at the time, but when he began to have regular epileptic fits, which lasted throughout his life, I felt that there was probably a connection.

TIP NUMBER 9 - one should always carefully supervise any interaction between youngsters and dogs, particularly if blunt instruments and hard balls are involved.

Ben attended approximately 800 cricket matches during his lifetime although he was lucky to survive that first season. Not only was he almost killed on May 30th, 1982, but we almost lost him less than two months later on July 24th thanks to my complacency. He followed me everywhere - or so I thought! Whilst I was busy organising my players and putting my kit in the changing rooms at South Godstone, which was about twenty miles away, Ben disappeared. The story is best told by this match report from the Worcester Park Playcricket website.

"On this particular Saturday in July 1982 Worcester Park were particularly strong and the Third Eleven Vice Captain Stemp decided to take a Fourth team into the back of beyond - well South Godstone anyway. And what a team it was for a Fourth XI. Did the Threes know that he had Geoff Johnson, Mike Trueman, Tony Humphreys and Neil Waller on board, plus the team's star mascot five month old Ben Stemp, a beautiful tri-colour Border Collie?

In a way Ben was responsible for the team's appalling performance.

The team had travelled the 20 or so miles to South Godstone in good time for a Saturday lunchtime and all arrived at the ground in plenty of time for the 2.30 start. The captain unloaded his gear, and with Ben running loose, he trudged up the slope with his bag to the pavilion. After changing into his whites he found Ben was missing. General panic ensued! Players went left and right calling for the dog but there was no sign.

On three sides the ground was surrounded by fields and woodlands whilst on the fourth side there was a housing estate and the busy A22, Eastbourne Road.

Still the team was there to play a game of cricket, not to look for a dog. It was agreed with the opposing skipper that Worcester Park should bat first, which from a cricketing point of view was not a good choice as this was in the days of using one new ball per game on a poorish looking wicket.

In the meantime Skipper Stemp had found a group of children in the woods to look for his dog and offered them a pound apiece if he were found. The kids took up the challenge enthusiastically and were soon to be heard making their way through the woods shouting "Ben! Ben!" at the top of their voices.

In a way this didn't help the batsmen either and the first 6 batsmen all fell for single figures with shouts from the woods of "Ben! Ben!" ringing in their ears. Mike Trueman, a genuine dog lover made an unaccustomed failure and admitted when he came off he was more worried about the dog than the cricket.

This was in the days before mobile phones and Skipper Stemp had had to drive down to the local hamlet where he was lucky enough to find a working call box. All he could do was ring the local police and ask for the number of the R.S.P.C.A. and return to the game and wait.

By the time he arrived back at the match seven wickets were down and it looked as though he might not even have time to change into his batting gear. Tony Humphreys, however, was putting up some dogged resistance and had been joined by young Glastonbury High School lad, Andy McKinnon. Just before the fall of the Doctor (Tony Humphreys Phd in gas) with the score on 79 an R.S.P.C.A. official arrived at the ground and gave the relieved skipper an address on the A22 where Ben could be found. He had apparently followed someone through the housing estate and had proceeded to walk along the busy A22 to the 'Lagham Arms'. On entering the pub, obviously lost, a woman decided to take him home and rang up the police. The woman already had three dogs and would quite happily have kept him if no-one claimed him.

Stemp threw off his pads and leapt into his car, not before, however, giving Neil Waller strict instructions not to get out before he returned. In fact Waller and McKinnon did survive until tea but the Park total was still abysmal (about 118). As young Andy had never before scored a fifty, Stemp made the decision to bat on after tea. (It was the only time he ever did that surprisingly enough). The decision was not, understandably, too popular with the opponents, but at the end of the day they still won easily enough.

Basically the Park team were relieved to have the dog back and merely went through the motions in the field."

Although Ben might not have known the rules of the game, he quickly began to realise that dogs and spectators were not allowed to cross the white line or boundary markers whilst a game was in progress. His behaviour soon became impeccable. He would lie there quietly watching the game until the players were applauded off the field, when he would start to bark his appreciation, before making a beeline to the tea room if it were the break between innings, to see what titbits he could beg.

The photograph below shows Ben in 1988 attending a cricket match at Worcester Park with a small group of my Sunday Third XI. From left to right they are Asif Malik, Malcolm Evans, Graham Bowers, Neil Waller and Martin Coleman. Malcolm, who was an electrician and general handyman, was responsible for building a dog flap in my conservatory thus making dog ownership much easier. Neil Waller was a fellow teacher at Glastonbury High School and Martin was one of our pupils.

Ben also suffered another cricket related injury at the hands of a youngster when my ten year old niece, Karen, and her seven year old brother, Matthew, stayed a week with me in 1992. Whilst visiting the cricket club, and unbeknown to me, Matthew trapped Ben's tail in the door of the scorebox. He only revealed his crime about twenty years later. It was several months before I noticed the kink in Ben's tail where I presume that it had been broken. The poor dog must have been in agony. Recently I have watched a video of Ben and the children which was taken later the same day. In it Matthew did seem to be showing more interest in Ben's tail than might seem normal. He was probably worried that the damage might have been noticeable.

Ben and Golf

In late 1981 John Murtagh, a fellow Glastonbury teacher, and myself became five day members of Cuddington Golf Club in Banstead. We used to rush up there regularly straight after school and play nine holes of golf. Ben was left at home to begin with as dogs did not really seem to be encouraged, and one did not wish to incur the displeasure of the Committee.

Ben's first encounter with golf, however, occurred on the top football pitch at Cheam Recreation Ground, which was about four hundred yards from my living room window. For about three months in Ben's first winter I took a pitching wedge and a tube of balls onto the Rec. to practice. I found out later, according to the bye-laws, that it was illegal, and I now confess to my crime, but there were usually very few witnesses at 7 a.m. in the morning.

On the first occasion of illegally practising golf on the Rec. I began by hitting the balls towards an open goal mouth at a distance of about a hundred yards. Initially Ben chased after the balls and brought them back. Eventually he decided that it was easier to pick each ball up when it landed and create a small pile by the goal post. I would then walk down to the pile of balls that Ben had gathered and hit them back towards the other goal so that Ben could repeat the process.

Ben was clever enough to make sure that he lay outside the line of fire. His eyesight must have been brilliant as thankfully I never hit him once.

Eventually I became confident enough of my position in the club to play a few holes with the dog. It also helped that the club appointed a much younger Head Professional in 1984, Mark Warner, a true dog lover.

Ben's behaviour was amazing from that very first day at Cuddington. Although he was kept on the lead the whole time, I made no attempt to tether him to the bag whenever I stopped to play a shot: I simply dropped the lead and told him to sit and wait. This behaviour was replicated at every tee and green. Ben was easily the most well behaved of all my canine golfing buddies.

As time elapses, memories have begun to fade of the happy times that we spent together on the golf course. Recently, however, whilst delving through some old papers I have come across a couple of items that have reminded me of the companionship that he gave me on the golf course.

In a 1989 diary, which was virtually unused, there was an extremely short entry for Boxing Day which blandly stated, "Played 9 with Ben." I also discovered a letter which I had written to my parents on March 10th, 1990, thanking them for a shirt which they had sent me for my birthday. The letter ended with the following P.S. "The weather is quite fine and I've taken Ben for three short walks after school on the golf course."

Ben and Bones

Although I did not brush Ben's teeth as often as I should have, they tended to be in quite good condition, which was probably the result of Ben's love of bones.

The rather faint photograph on the right shows Ben in the undergrowth at the bottom of the garden guarding one of his favourite bones, which I tended to buy from the pet shop in Worcester Park, and which littered both the house and garden. They were unusually large and heavy and I was reliably informed that they were camel bones.

When those bones were new they used to be full of delicious marrow which took hours of determined chewing to extract. Even when there was no more marrow left, Ben continued to work upon the bones rather like an ancient sailor creating an intricate piece of scrimshaw from a whale bone.

After my earlier experience with Laddie, several years before, who would attack me if I came close to his food, I was determined that I did not want Ben to be that sort of dog. From an early age I would occasionally lift his food bowl to my face or pretend to chew his bone. As a result he came to realise that I did not present a threat. In fact he was quite happy to pass over his bone whenever asked.

Ben, Balls and Frisbees

Ben loved playing with a ball, from the very first day that I threw a ball on a rope. I quickly found that he was happy to race around me in a large circle, waiting for the ball to be thrown. He would sprint after it, catch it and then drop it at my feet, before starting to circle me again. There was no need to train him to do that. I felt that he often got more exercise in ten minutes of ball chasing than most dogs would get in a two hour walk.

Ben was also extremely adept at catching a frisbee but unfortunately the frisbees that we used were often the hard plastic ones which his teeth cut into, thus making the edge slightly jagged, which in turn cut either his tongue or gums. If ever the frisbee returned with a bloody rim, I immediately abandoned play.

TIP NUMBER 11 - it is better to use a soft rubber frisbee than a hard plastic one.

Apart from having great eye-mouth coordination Ben was also quite adept at using his nose to either head a ball or to push a ball around. I always had to be careful if ever I saw a game of football on the Rec. as Ben always wanted to be involved. If it was an informal kick-around by a group of children I used to let him play for a short while as his dribbling skill was quite impressive to watch, and seemed to entertain both the players and any spectators who happened to be watching

Ben and Presents

During his lifetime Ben acquired hundreds of presents not only from me but from a variety of friends. There were random presents such as a large juicy bone or a cuddly toy which were often impulse buys whenever the pet shop was visited, and then there were the more formal presents, which tended to be wrapped, which marked his birthday or Christmas, and as he lived for over sixteen years there were a lot of them.

The rather blurry photograph on the right shows Ben proudly carrying one of his unwrapped Christmas presents. Eventually he would lie down and grip the present with his paws before turning the wrapping paper into confetti which unfortunately I had to clear up.

He was surprisingly caring towards his toys and would often carry his favourite cuddly toy of the moment around with him, or run about excitedly squeaking a cheap rubber hedgehog in his mouth. What was really surprising is that he seemed to know most of the soft toys such as the teddy bear or monkey by name and could find them when asked to do so.

The photograph on the left shows some of his favourite toys. Some of them such as the Monkey or the Floppy Dog, Ben had had for several years. The monkey on the right of the photograph was easily his favourite toy and he used to walk around proudly with it in his mouth offering it occasionally to amused watchers. The Floppy Dog on the left of the photograph, with its long loose limbs and ears was great to shake.

As I did not have the heart to throw away Ben's favourite toys when they became torn and dirty, I ended up having to gently wash them and make any necessary repairs. The Monkey, minus his squeak, was stitched up on numerous occasions whilst the Floppy Dog had to have at least one leg and ear re-attached.

Despite the fact that Ben had a box in which his toys were supposed to be kept, more often than not they would end up littering almost every room in the house. He was like an untidy child, who would take his toys out of the box to play with them but never tidied them away.

Although he was not short of toys, Ben was not averse to helping himself to other people's property especially if they were careless enough to leave their slippers lying around. The photo on the previous page shows him gently chewing a slipper of one of my female lodgers. As I have never had any pink slippers, I obviously found it more amusing to photograph him rather than stop him.

Ben and Friends

As the house in Netley Close had four bedrooms it enabled me to occasionally let out rooms to help pay the mortgage and household bills. One condition for any lodger to be accepted was that they had to meet with Ben's approval.

Ben soon became used to seeing a rapid turnover of guests, such as foreign exchange students, French or German language assistants, overseas cricketers who were hired by Worcesterr Park Cricket Club, or tennis players who were involved in competitions at Sutton Tennis and Squash Club. Ben made them all welcome.

Some members of the household, however, were more permanent. The longest lasting lodger was Denise Tierney, the lady on the right, who was a P.E. teacher at Sutton Common Girls School, aka Glenthorne, which was the sister school of Glastonbury H.S. She had had the privilege of renting a room from me in Brandy Way in 1980. When she found out that I was moving in 1981 she wondered whether she would have to find a new place to live. I put her mind at rest, however, by saying that I needed her to help me move, as I had a bad back. She was much stronger than me, plus she was very reliable!

In total Denise stayed with me for nine years until I rented a short stay room to Nick Ormsby, Bob's twin brother, and within a short period of time they married, on April 8th 1988, at St. John's Church, Welling. Denise was almost like a sister to me and a mother figure to Ben.

Another guest who stayed at the house, in 1982, was Suzi Stuttard, a lass from Todmorden, who apart from having a day job often sang with a band in a hotel at weekends. I can not say that I really approve of dogs being dressed up but the photograph on the left really shows how soft Ben was.

One Saturday evening I took Suzi and her boyfriend, Harvey, to a party at an ex-pupil's house in South Sutton. Whilst she went to get a drink I asked him what he did for a living. He said that he played a guitar. Feeling that he had not really understood my question I said, "But what do you really do for a living."

His answer rather floored me when he said that he played in a band called Hot Chocolate. I must say that I felt rather stupid as the group had had an enormous hit that year with "It Started with a Kiss."

I learned later that the guitarist was Harvey Hinsley, who apparently forgave my ignorance and invited a group of us over to his house on a private estate in Ewell to play snooker the following day. Suzi, who had always wanted to be a songwriter collaborated with him in 1987 to write another Hot Chocolate hit 'Never Pretend'.

Ben was an exceptionally sociable dog and enjoyed being included in all our activities. He was also exceedingly photographic as can be seen in this Christmas picture which was taken in 1982 when he was ten months old, with Suzi and her friends Reza and Louise. He is certainly the most sober looking individual there.

Probably the most cheerful lodger and a lady who got on extremely well with Ben was Dawn, a teacher who taught with Denise at Sutton Common/Glenthorne High School. I have spoken to Denise recently and neither of us can remember her surname nor the subject that she taught. Although Dawn only stayed at Chez Stemp for about three months in 1988 she made a lasting impression as she was responsible for re-covering the four dining room chairs with a fawn coloured material, which still graces the chairs over thirty years later.

The photograph on the left is one of several that I have of Dawn and Ben who became very good friends over a short period of time.

After the lovely Dawn left she sent a very sweet thankyou card, which simply said "To David & Ben, Thankyou for letting me share your home, Love from Dawn x"

There is quite a good view of the bottom half of the house behind Ben and Dawn, before the largish porch was built in 1994. The lower section of the window above the front door had been blocked up by a board when I first moved into the house. I removed it primarily so that Ben could look out, which has proved a boon for all my furry friends.

The rather hazy looking photograph on the right shows Ben lying under the cloth, which covered a bar billiards table which resided in the front room for a couple of years. Ben was obviously watching me take his photograph. The apparent poor quality of the picture was basically the result of Ben's wet nose leaving a trail of dried nasal mucus upon the inside of the glass. Trying to remove the 'nose art' from that small area of glass has been a problem now for over forty years.

Another of the lodgers who had a great affect upon both Ben and myself was a rather dipsy, bespectacled middle aged lady called Margaret Tetlow, from Nottingham, who worked for Royal Doulton at Peter Jones' store in Chelsea, before moving to a store in Epsom. The photograph of Margaret on the left of the page shows Margaret hugging Ben at the top of the stairs. Although it looks as though he is being strangled, Ben loved the attention.

In comparison to the majority of residents in the house who tended to favour tracksuits and jeans, Margaret usually looked so prim and proper and always went to work in a smart suit, as befitted her line of work. Her strong Midland's accent, however, did not quite synch with her appearance, nor did some of the turns of phrase that she used. The most memorable examples of her rather idiosyncratic vocabulary was that she always referred to Ben's ears as 'tabs' and would often exclaim that he was 'melting' when in fact he was moulting.

Margaret was a very friendly person who tended to get on with most people. I think that my mother thought that she would make an ideal daughter-in-law. These two photographs show her on the left with my mother and below with my mother's cousin, Bessie Naylor. They stayed at the house for a week in 1988 when I went to play in a Bridge Tournament in Torquay.

Margaret stayed at Chez Stemp for about three or four years and, although she regularly criticised the state of the house, we were extremely sad when she left as she had been an exceptionally trustworthy and tidy lodger who was brilliant with Ben. I always think of what Margaret would have said if ever I fail to empty the washing up bowl in the kitchen sink overnight.

Unfortunately Margaret fell out with another short term lodger, a fledgling chiropractor from Cork who, apart from being untidy, had an exaggerated sense of her own importance. As a result Margaret invested nearly all her savings into a one roomed studio flat in South Sutton in 1990. It was an very bad move. We had lost an extremely good lodger and, no sooner had she bought the flat, than there was a housing price slump and poor Margaret suffered from negative equity for years.

Ben and I used to visit her some Sunday lunchtimes if ever we visited the tennis club. The photograph on the right shows Ben and Margaret in her rather smart and tidy studio flat.

On the day that Margaret left our house I was at work. When I returned I found an envelope addressed to David/Ben which merely said "Keys in Envolop. Thanks for letting me stop here. Love Marg. Will give you a ring when I am on phone." On the back of the envelope in large letters it merely said "Look After Ben."

The final long term tenant who met Ben, and arrived in 1997, was a twenty-five year old South African from Johannesburg called Colin Ritchie, who worked in computers. At first I was reluctant to accept him because of his age, but it transpired that he was much more serious than I was. Having served in the South African army he was very disciplined and tidy and he loved animals, although I was not too keen upon Sid, his pet snake, or the frozen mice in the freezer. His main hobby was repairing and racing minis which he kept with a trailer in the driveway.

Ben also welcomed to our home several tennis players who competed in the annual satellite tournaments which were held at Sutton Tennis and Squash Club. Some of the most famous stars of English tennis appeared in these events. I remember on one occasion, probably in 1985, that I was due to look after two up and coming young tennis stars. Clean sheets had been put on the beds and extra food had been purchased. The first player, James Turner, appeared at about 5 pm. He was extremely pleasant and seemed very satisfied with everything that had been provided. He went on to play at Wimbledon in the singles twice and in the Doubles four times.

We waited quite a long time for the other player, James's occasional Doubles partner, to appear before we ate. Andrew Castle, who became the England Number 1 tennis player in 1986, was the no-show. I must admit that I was more than a little annoyed, not because I had prepared a bed and food for him or because he had failed to notify me, but because I had to forfeit the £7 fee for his upkeep.

Ben and I had another unexpected encounter with an even more famous tennis player in the mid to late 80s. It occurred one sunny day in July whilst I was playing cricket for Worcester Park Sunday Third XI at Lensbury. Ben was watching intently whilst our team were fielding. I had just come on to bowl when the batsman pulled away as there was someone walking in front of the sight screen behind my arm. It was Jimmy Connors who was walking towards the tennis courts at Lensbury to practice for the upcoming Wimbledon tournament. He might have been a great tennis player but he was obviously not au fait with the etiquette deemed appropriate upon the cricket field.

In 1992 Clinton and Barbara Kempnich stayed for three or four months in the summer. Clinton had been brought over from Queensland to play cricket for Worcester Park Cricket Club. His season did not go too well as he was dropped by the First Eleven and Barbara badly injured her leg. In the end they decided to curtail his season and went travelling around Europe.

Clinton concentrated upon coaching when he returned to Australia and became the Director of Junior Coaching at his club, Valley District C.C., for whom he still plays, when not playing for the Queensland Over 60s team.

Ben and I also opened our home on a handful of occasions to overseas students who were forwarded to us by the International Student Organisation. One of the first was Yann Carton, a schoolboy from Dakar in Senegal, who stayed with us in July, 1986. It was not easy keeping an athletic fifteen year old occupied for three weeks, particularly when he was probably used to a better standard of life in Dakar where his father was a shipowner and he had servants at his beck and call. My main criticism of him, however, which I recorded in a diary entry, was that he was a late riser and slightly unpunctual.

Amongst the various activities that I laid on for Yann was a trip to Lensbury where he went swimming and boating whilst I played cricket. We also went to the Tennis club on a couple of occasions where Yann managed to play a few games of tennis and squash. Of more interest to Ben, however, was a trip to Box Hill which was always entertaining.

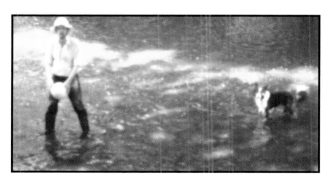

This small photograph was taken earlier that year on a Glastonbury High School Geography field trip, which was basically an excuse to frolic in the River Mole besides the Stepping Stones before scrambling up and down the steep Chalk escarpment.

It was easier and more enjoyable looking after girls. The photograph on the right is of two Danish girls, Julie Kurland and Malene Linde who stayed for a week in 1988 while they attended a summer school at Cheam High School. I provided them with bed and breakfast. After they returned to Bagsvaerd they wrote a charming thank-you letter in which they thanked me for my hospitality and said that "We miss you and your dog."

The car behind them was my white Fiat UNO which replaced the Panda which I had when I first acquired Ben. I replaced the UNO with a Nissan Micra Passion in 1997 when Ben was fifteen. One of the first things I did with that car was to remove the front passenger seat to help Ben access the car. The things one does for ones dog!

As both my parents had retired in1981, they became regular visitors whenever they visited my grandmother in Cranleigh.

I recently discovered this photo of my mother and Ben on Cheam Rec, amongst some of my father's slides. It must have been taken in 1982 as Ben looks exceptionally young.

There were several more mature students who stayed at Chez Stemp in the 1990s. One of the most memorable was a very pleasant American student called Mick Flanagan who came from St. Mary's College, Minnesota, for the Spring Term in 1994 to study at a college in the City. As thanks for letting him stay he gifted me a wooden decoy duck, which I still have on display.

On several occasions I was asked by Stanley Park High School if I could look after a Language Assistant for about nine months. Two of them, Ellen Frenz and Tobias Muhlpointner, who both came from Germany, became good friends with Ben and myself over their short time with me. We still exchange letters every Christmas, although a quarter of a century has elapsed. Tobi, who was a high ranking Handball player in Germany, even tried his hand at cricket. His bowling, however, which was really a throw, was quite frightening to face.

Tobi thought the world of Ben and was extremely saddened following his death in 1998. The accompanying photograph shows Tobi paying his respects besides Ben's grave.

Ben - the instigator of home improvement

Ben really was a very costly dog as, apart from his daily upkeep and the numerous vet bills, many of the alterations to the house which were carried out during his lifetime were undertaken with his welfare in mind.

One of the first major alterations to the property was to install a good security system in 1983, not to protect my vast collection of cricket books, but to protect my most valuable possession, Ben himself. I was probably panicked into buying the system, from the father of one of my pupils, by tales of dog-napping in Nonsuch Park, and, as it was in the days before dogs were supposed to be micro-chipped, a good security system afforded some level of protection.

By 1991 I was completely disenchanted by having to leave a pile of old towels just inside the front door of the house so that I could attempt to dry a wet dog. I took the plunge and had a large porch built at the front of the house so that I had plenty of room to store the towels and dry Ben. One could even leave him there to thoroughly dry out before allowing him in the house.

I was that pleased with the way that the porch helped with the process of keeping spatters of mud out of the house that, two years later in May 1993, I spent a fortune on double glazing the whole of the house and building quite a large brick based Victorian conservatory at the rear of the property. The photo on the right shows an elderly Ben lying upon the lawn in front of the conservatory.

For a glorified dog kennel it was the height of luxury as it was carpeted, had good lighting and had some extremely comfortable garden furniture. There was only one problem, Ben did not really seem to like it. If he was shut in there he would bark or scratch the PVC door until he was let into the main building. Those marks are still visible.

Bathtime for Ben

Keeping Ben clean was an onerous but necessary task if one wanted to keep ones home in a reasonable state of cleanliness. Fortunately there was a hose pipe at the side of the house which enabled me to give him a dousing down for his legs, tail and under-carriage every time we encountered muddy conditions in the park. No matter how long one spent upon hosing him down, however, seemed to completely clean him, as was evidenced by the state of the towels which were used to dry him and upon the dirty marks upon the staircase.

Life became much easier after the conservatory was built as Ben could be given a cursory hosing and towelling down before being left in there to dry off completely. A couple of hours later any dried mud that remained could be removed with a stiff bristle brush.

On certain occasions a hosing down was not sufficient, particularly if he had engaged in that most disgusting of canine habits of rolling in fox poo. Then the only real course of action to eliminate the foul smell was to give him a bath, which could be a time consuming, unpleasant experience for both of us.

It was fortunate that I had managed to give Ben a couple of baths and got him accustomed to the hair drier when he was very small. When he became older and heavier bath-time was not an experience to be enjoyed as he was always on the lookout to escape the soapy water. The more he struggled, the more he floundered, causing waves of water to wash over the side of the bath.

The heavy plastic shower curtain had to be pulled tightly shut if ever I left the side of the bath or else he would leap out and shake violently, spraying water all over the bathroom. Bath-time was usually such a wet experience, therefore, that I found it best to strip to the waist before embarking upon the mission.

When Ben was eleven he was diagnosed with dermatitis and alopecia which meant that I had to bath him in a special medicated shampoo every week, for two or three months. That was a nightmare for both of us, especially as I had to wear rubber gloves and rub the shampoo into his skin so that he was covered in lather. He then had to be left in the bath for ten minutes before showering him off.

Ben put me off bathing dogs for life! He had more baths than all my other dogs put together. Benji and Gemma had perhaps one a year, whilst Poppi had none as she would have bitten me if I had attempted to pick her up to put her in the bath, whilst Sophie had a couple of baths when very young which seemed to put her off bathing for life. The mere mention of the word 'bath' was enough to make her run away and hide. For most of my dogs, therefore, a cold shower and a brush was the order of the day and, if truth is to be told, they usually looked immaculate.

TIP NUMBER 11 - if one has to bathe a dog, a rubber mat on the bottom of the bath will stop the dog sliding around and panicking.

Ben's dodgy tummy

Throughout his life Ben had regular outbreaks of diarrhoea and Colitis, which was not pleasant for either of us and necessitated frequent trips to see our favourite vet Nick Dodds of the Dodds and Phillips Veterinarian practice in Churchill Road, where we would be given either anti-biotics and/or a probiotic paste and advice to feed him bland food such as chicken and rice until he was better. Occasionally I must admit that I self-medicated him with a little Kaolin and Morphine, which sometimes worked and was cheaper.

Part of the problem I feel was down to my own ignorance of canine nutrition. I like to think that I have learnt from my mistakes with Ben and have at last stumbled upon a diet which has almost completely eliminated a bad stomach, although it is always useful to have a tube of Pro-Kolin nearby.

Much of the problem, however, was due to Ben's unhygienic scavenging behaviour which, try as I might, I never managed to control completely whenever he was off the lead. If ever there was a dirty animal bone in the park, deposited by one of the numerous foxes which frequent the place, Ben was sure to find it. He also had the disgusting habit of occasionally licking the spot where another dog had urinated. I tried fitting him with a canvas muzzle but that did not work as he could still lick. I even tried stitching an old sock over the end of the muzzle, which although it worked looked cruel. The most reliable method was to keep him on the lead. The photograph on the right shows one unhappy dog.

Even the garden was not a completely safe, disease-free environment for Ben as, apart from nocturnal visits there by cats and foxes, the seeds which were scattered around the bird feeders by the numerous sparrows which visited the garden in those days, also attracted a host of pigeons to spread their poo around.

TIP NUMBER 12 - if one wants a bird feeder, why not invest in one with a circular tray beneath to catch the seed and poo.

Ben, Cats and Foxes

For the first four or five years of his life Ben appeared to hate both cats and foxes. He would bark frenetically if ever he spotted one as he looked through the window, and would chase them whenever possible. The back garden was virtually a cat and fox free zone.

Next door, however, there was a plot of land upon which had been built, by an old retired engineer, several rusty delipidated corrugated iron sheds that had long ago surrendered to the ravages of the natural world. The sheds made a wonderful place for cats to shelter from the weather and made great dens for the foxes. On several occasions I was actually able, through the side window of my house, to video fox cubs at play in the undergrowth between the sheds.

On the other side of my property, my neighbour Geoff Ward had a luxurious garden. At the bottom of that garden, next to my fence was a tiny rickety garden shed, the roof of which was shaded by an overhanging tree. Foxes regularly used the roof of Geoff's shed as a place on which to sleep during the day time. Their strong musty odour regularly attracted Ben's frustrated interest. He would stand on his hind legs, to his full height, against the shed and occasionally bark but the fox would studiously ignore him.

Sometimes the foxes would become even bolder. On one occasion I filmed a vixen and one of her cubs sunbathing upon my lawn for about twenty minutes. The vixen spent much of her time preening the fur of her youngster. The rather hazy photograph on the right was taken from that video.

As for cats, however, one day something really strange happened that altered Ben's attitude towards them. I was talking to a couple of neighbours at the end of my drive and Ben was standing idly by, waiting to go for a walk. Suddenly, under the fence from the wilderness next door, there emerged a slim black cat which was purring loudly. It walked straight up to Ben and rubbed its body against the bewildered dog, before rubbing itself against the legs of the small group of people whilst still purring. The cat, whose collar provided the information that he was called Sooty, showed no fear, only friendship.

We saw Sooty a few times after that and then, as quickly as he had appeared, he disappeared. I never found out where he came from or what happened to him but he certainly had had a profound influence upon Ben. From that day onwards Ben no longer seemed to see cats as the enemy and tended to ignore them.

The photograph on the right, which was also taken from a video, shows Ben walking across the small front lawn, about to cock his leg over a rose bush, totally ignoring Oscar, the cat of my next door neighbour.

Ben the perfect passenger

For sixteen years Ben rode shotgun in three different cars, each of which had a dog friendly feature. The Fiat Panda which I had bought in April 1982, a month before Ben came into my life, had obviously been bought in preparation for buying a dog as it had a long canvas roof that could be either fully or partially rolled back, thus allowing good ventilation for the dog when parked. The main flaw with that car, however, was the fact that shortly after buying the vehicle, whilst driving to Cranleigh at about 50 miles per hour, the sunroof was ripped from it moorings with a frightening roar, scaring both the puppy and myself. It took a solicitor's letter, which resulted in £150 compensation, and over six months for the fault to be rectified.

Four years later in July 1986, I landed myself in debt by buying a brand new Fiat Uno S60 Carte Blanche. As the interest on the debt was 0% I splashed out on a glass sunroof for the car. If ever I left the dog in the car I made sure that the sunroof was open and perhaps a couple of windows were slightly ajar to create a through breeze.

I loved the Uno and kept it for over eleven years until just after the death of Princess Diana. I do not know whether it was the fact that the police were trying to trace a white Fiat Uno which had been seen in the vicinity of the accident or not, but I sold it in October 1997 in part exchange for a Renault Micra Passion which also had a sunroof, and which I further adapted for my now elderly dog by removing the passenger seat.

TIP NUMBER 13 - buy a car with a sunroof as leaving a dog in a car in hot weather with no ventilation can be fatal. It is also advisable to park in the shade and leave the windows slightly ajar.

For much of the time Ben sat on the front passenger seat where he would sit bolt upright, for the first twenty minutes or so, watching where we were going before settling down for a snooze. The deep throated roar of a passing motorbike, however, always grabbed his attention and made me wonder whether he had been a biker in a previous life.

At the start of our travels together neither of us wore a seat belt as until January 31st, 1983, the wearing of seat belts was not compulsory. As someone who had possessed a driving licence for twenty years, and had been a passenger for the previous eighteen years, I must admit that I felt rather aggrieved at having to "clunk click" for every trip. I was, however, extremely concerned about the safety of my dog and always drove more carefully whenever he was on the front seat, as I was aware that if I halted suddenly he would be catapulted forward and might be severely injured or, if he were on the back seat he might injure either myself or my passenger.

In over forty years of driving with a dog, or dogs onboard I have never once been pulled up or fined for speeding. I do have harnesses for the dogs although I must admit that for short, everyday journeys I am usually too lazy to belt them up.

TIP NUMBER 14 - it is advisable to buy an RAC approved harness through which a seat belt can be easily passed to protect the dog or passengers in case of an emergency stop or accident.

Apart from the daily short journeys to and from school, the golf club or the cricket club, Ben and I used to drive about 250 miles north to visit my parents about three or four times a year. They had both decided to retire in 1981 and moved to St. Annes-on-Sea, where my mother had inherited, from her Aunt Florrie, a beautiful bungalow which backed on to the Royal Lytham and St. Annes Golf Club.

Ben was in his element at my parents' home as there was a largish enclosed back garden with a beautiful manicured lawn surrounded by flower and vegetable beds through which he was at liberty to wander. As the backdoor was usually open he spent most of his time out there, although nothing could compare with standing on a plush comfortable armchair to watch the traffic passing by, through the blinds in the front room.

The visits to St. Annes usually entailed frequent long walks. Most of the mornings began with a very early stroll across the golf course looking for golf balls before any players had emerged, whilst the afternoons were often spent exploring the sand dunes down by the beach. Occasionally a longer walk would ensue if we trekked towards Blackpool or walked around Fairhaven Lake with my parents.

The favourite part of the visit for me, however, was to visit some of the haunts of my youth around Nelson, which also entailed quite a lot of walking. Recently I watched a video which I had taken in 1991 of Ben and I walking across a wind-swept moor at Sabden before climbing Pendle Hill. There were sheep all around but Ben appeared to be completely disinterested in them. The photograph on the right was taken of Ben at Sabden. His ears and tail were erect and he looked to be enjoying himself.

Occasionally we would drive over to Darwen to visit my brother Bill, his wife June, and their four children Paul, Neil, Karen and Matthew. That tended to be quite boring for Ben as he was not allowed in the house as June was allergic to dogs, which tablets helped to eradicate when they eventually bought a dog. Ben probably enjoyed the numerous walks that we made to the Victorian tower which dominates the moors, more than being confined to the car every time we visited Darwen.

Ben must also have accompanied me on the fifty mile round trip to Cranleigh on several hundred occasions to visit three or four of my father's family who still lived there. The most important of these relatives was my ancient grandmother, who was already 84 years old when I acquired Ben. She was quite a recluse who rarely left her small semi-detached cottage even to walk down the garden, following the death of her husband in 1965. Her lack of physical activity meant that she lost the ability to walk without the aid of a zimmer frame for at least the last twenty five years of her life. She did, however, enjoy visits from Ben and myself.

My grandmother remained in the cottage until 1994, when at the age of 96 she went to live in St. Annes with my widowed father for six more years, before dying at the age of 102. The photograph on the right shows Ben visiting them both at St. Annes.

The photograph on the left, which was taken in August 1988, shows a quizzical looking Ben in my grandmother's small but overgrown garden in Cranleigh. The corrugated sheeting behind him was about all that remained of the chicken coop and run which used to house several hens when my grandfather was alive, and had provided a constant supply of fresh eggs.

Because the garden was neglected by my grandmother, however, it had become a miniature wildlife haven with delicious wild strawberries and swarms of butterflies and bees, toads and frogs and nests of mice and rats. For Ben the garden provided a constant stream of interesting smells and wildlife to watch.

Next door to my grandmother's house was the home of an elderly couple Harold Edward (aka Jim) and Phoebe Port, who usually made quite a fuss of Ben as they had owned a string of Border Collies. Jim had been a groundsman who worked on the ground at both Cranleigh Cricket Club and at Cranleigh School. One of the tales that Jim told showed the intelligence of the breed and their devotion to their master.

On one occasion Jim had walked the half mile to the cricket ground with his dog, who always accompanied him. When Jim arrived there he realised that he had forgotten his tobacco pouch. Rather than walk home and back again, he scribbled a note to his wife and attached it to the dog's collar. The dog did not really want to leave his master but eventually understood what he had to do and returned home, where Phoebe gave him the tobacco pouch to take back to Jim.

What is really amazing about that story is that the dog either had to go across the Common and then over the bridge, or had to cross the railway line. Which ever way the dog went he had to negotiate two or three roads and a railway line, which posed a certain degree of danger even fifty years ago.

My grandmother's garden, however, was nothing in comparison to that of my father's cousin, Dawn, who lived in a seventeenth century detached cottage in Wanborough Lane, Cranleigh, with her retired husband, an ex-solicitor, Geoff Garland. Their garden was much larger and consisted of a large lawn surrounded by a variety of trees and flower beds, next to which was a small orchard. The garden also contained a variety of animals which Ben rarely encountered in every day life such as free range chickens, quail, a variety of ducks, a donkey and tethered goats, plus a small pond with several colourful koi carp.

As soon as Ben entered the garden he would move swiftly along the crazy paving path to an alcove beside the front door which contained an ancient bird cage. The photograph on the right shows him standing upon his hind legs to stare at the budgerigar in the cage, before turning his attention to the rabbit in its hutch.

As with the sheep on the moor Ben tended to ignore the chickens and the donkey in the garden. My only worry was when he wandered within five yards of a large goat, with a pair of exceedingly sharp looking horns, which gave him a fixed look. It still impresses me when I look at the video of the encounter at Ben's comprehension of the spoken word. I spoke quite calmly and merely said, "No don't go near it, Ben! Come away! Yes!" Whereupon he turned upon his heel, cocked his leg over
a plant and wandered away. The photograph on the right shows that goat which was on a sturdy chain which allowed him to move three yards from the post. His tiny, sharp, pointed horns are only just visible.

Ben and 'Three Acres and a Cow'

Much of my life in the early 1990s was spent in Record Offices, Libraries or Museums in Guildford, Woking, Winchester, Chichester, Kew or Horsham doing research upon the Hamshire family, as I was intent upon writing a book about my great, great grandfather, Eli Hamshire, who believed that if everyone had three acres and a cow then poverty would be eliminated. Ben patiently accompanied me upon most of these trips and, as a result, spent hours on end cooped up in my Fiat Uno.

I had then, using Windows 95, to transfer all my notes onto my computer to create a best selling book, in the Cranleigh area. All this deprived Ben of my company for numerous more hours as he waited patiently outside my office. I felt that guilty about my neglect of him that I dedicated 'Three Acres and a Cow - the Life and Works of Eli Hamshire' to my faithful companion.

The photograph on the right is the one that I chose as the frontispiece for the book. It was taken in the dining room of my parent's bungalow in St. Annes. Sitting in the dark to the left of the dog is my mother who died in 1991, which means that Ben was probably about six or seven years old when the picture was taken. Two large copies of this photograph were framed and given to my grandmother and parents.

Following the self publication of the book I then embarked upon a very extensive selling campaign, which led to me visiting most of the bookshops in Surrey and West Sussex. On one of these trips Ben showed his lack of use as a guard dog when he allowed a thief to steal a box of books from the boot of the car. I can not believe that the thief realised that he was stealing sixteen copies of 'Three Acres and a Cow'.

It was while researching the book that I discovered another branch of the family who were still living in Gadbridge Lane, Ewhurst, on the site of Eli Hamshire's original three acre small-holding. Carol Woodrow, née Hamshire, who was a great grand-daughter of Eli, lived there in a small semi-detached cottage with her daughter Rebecca and her two beautiful Border Collies, Kerry and Tramp. Kerry is in the foreground in the photograph on the right which does not really do them justice.

Tramp was extremely large for a Border Collie and must have weighed at least 25 kilograms, although his beautiful fluffy tricolour coat probably made him look even larger. He was a very gentle, friendly character who was easily dominated by his sister, Kerry, who used to prevent him from sleeping upstairs.

On the other side of Gadbridge Lane there were a couple of oldish semi-detached houses surrounded by a paddock and a series of large sheds, which had been the site of Eli Hamshire's thriving chicken farm. Breeding chickens in Ewhurst and selling them in Guildford and the surrounding villages had made Eli quite a fortune in the nineteenth century. These houses were occupied by two grandchildren of Eli Hamshire, Freda and Allen. Allen was Carol's father who lived there with her step mother Rosemary and his son David.

Whilst, as a researcher, it was fantastic to find descendants of Eli Hamshire still living upon land that had been owned by the great man himself in the late nineteenth century, what was more interesting to me, however, was their beautiful trio of Border Collies:; Penny, Chrissie and Dan.

Allen's wife, Rosemary, has had over sixty years' experience of both breeding and training Border Collies, and her living room has numerous photographs of some of her prize winning dogs and their rosettes, which they have won for their obedience and agility at dog shows up and down the country.

I must admit that I was rather envious of her control over her dogs, although it does help that she has a large paddock next to the house, which is well stocked with all the necessary agility equipment such as jumps, hoops, tunnels, A-frame and poles for the dogs to weave around.

Allen's favourite dog was undoubtedly Dan, whom he would get to sit patiently with a pipe in his mouth and a cap upon his head. What I found most interesting about Dan was the fact that his left eye was brown and his right eye was blue, which led to him often being referred to as 'Blue Dan'. If one looks very closely at the accompanying photograph one should be able to spot the difference.

The photograph below, which was taken in the early 1990s, shows six siblings who were all offspring of Rosemary's dog Tessa. Kerry and Tramp are on the left.

Ben - The Final Chapter

By the time he reached the age of fourteen Ben was no longer the young dog, whom I had loved, who impressed people with his catching and footballing skills. In a way he was a different dog, a wise and noble creature, whose features were now tinged with grey and whose coat looked remarkably unkempt. In his heart, however, he was still a young dog who loved to play a game of catch with a tennis ball and would occasionally head a football.

Although he was no longer as agile Ben could still climb the two flights of stairs to sleep outside my bedroom door at night time. The photograph on the left shows a much younger Ben preparing to go to sleep outside my bedroom door and blocking the use of the room behind him. He chose to sleep upon the relatively hard carpet rather than in his soft bed in the kitchen.

One of the downsides of owning an old dog such as Ben was the fact that he became slightly incontinent towards the end of his life and his favourite resting places were lined with plastic sheeting and old blankets. I even tried fitting him with an improvised towelling nappy.

I loved old Ben just as much as I had loved the younger one, despite his mounting health problems. Looking back through his file makes me realise how fortunate I had been to take out Life Cover on Ben with Petplan. For his final year the cover only cost £264.07. It makes one realise how the cost of veterinarian care has rocketed in the past twenty five years, as I have just paid £988 for ten year old Sophie's annual cover and she is rarely ill.

During his final fourteen months several claims were put in to Petplan, for which they paid out over £1,100, for hypothyroid treatment, removal of tumours, an anal adenoma operation, plus five claims for colitis and four for arthritis, from which he must have suffered quite badly, as on one occasion when he was mounting the stairs he turned round and snapped at me when I touched his hind quarters. That was the only time in over sixteen years that he ever showed any sign of aggression towards me.

Ben's medical file reveals what a sickly dog he must have been, and how much we both owed to the medical skill of our vet, Nick Dodds. In the first five months of 1996, statements from Petplan revealed that they had paid out on three occasions for 'vomiting'. Although all my other dogs have been sick on occasions, I can not remember any of them requiring medical attention for this condition. The photograph on the previous page was taken in the park outside my house and shows my desperate attempt to keep an elderly Ben safe from picking up any item which might make him sick.

As we entered the month of May, 1998, it was obvious that the end was quite near. I tried to carry on with life as much as normal but feared the worst. On May 9th I took Ben to watch the Third XI and myself play against Addiscombe at the ground that we rented from Old Tiffinians which Ben knew well. Following our victory we went for a drink at our clubhouse in Worcester Park. I have a lasting memory of our team sitting around drinking, whilst Ben ended up standing in the midst of a group of four, five and six year old children who were playing football all around him. He loved children!

The following Saturday another event occurred at a cricket match which left a lasting impression upon me, as it showed the ignorance of some people regarding dogs. We had travelled to play at Normandy, near Guildford, where Ben had behaved impeccably. As we walked back to the car, Ben who was plodding along very unsteadily, passed close to a small boy who was obviously very scared of dogs and screamed. The father became very irate and said that I should have better control over my dog - a dog who posed absolutely no danger to any other living being.

The next day another cricket/dog related incident occurred which again left a sour taste in my mouth. It was a warm Sunday when our team visited Dundonald Rec. in Merton to play Carshalton. I parked in the shade in a tree lined avenue with both the windows and the sunroof ajar. Ben was quite happy sleeping on the rear seat with a bowl of water sitting where the front seat used to exist, before I had removed it to help him access the car.

We were just knocking up when some know-it-all neighbour came over to complain that there was a dog locked in a car, and he was going to ring up the R.S.P.C.A. and the police if the owner left it there. I tried to explain to the man that the car was in the shade with the windows open and that the dog loved being in the car, but one can not argue with some people, for as Alexander Pope (1709) said "A little learning is a dangerous thing."

As a result I had to tether Ben beneath a bench which was the only shade that I could find. It was certainly warmer there and nowhere near as comfortable as lying on the back seat of the car.

On the Monday I took Ben a short walk in the morning before going in to school. By that stage I was working part time and had the afternoons free, and so was able to return at lunchtime. Ben seemed to be breathing a little heavier but I was not worried enough to contact the vet. By the evening, however, he seemed to be in some discomfort and whined occasionally. As he could still handle the stairs I made up a bed for him on the floor of my bedroom and spent most of the night comforting him as he was obviously in pain.

The following morning I made an appointment with the vet. Unfortunately Nick was on holiday and so we were seen by his partner Jenny Phillips and the head nurse Barbara Byrne. Jenny was very sympathetic and felt that there was little that could be done, and said that it would be a kindness to put him out of his misery. After watching him suffer the previous night I reluctantly agreed and held him gently as Jenny administered his final injection. He gave a little gasp and then passed away in my arms.

The photograph on the right is the last one of him ever taken, a few days before his death with his coat looking shiny and shaggy, and a great look of wisdom and contentedness upon his face. Perhaps he realised that his life was virtually over and the pain that he felt would be no more.

His body was wrapped in a blanket and I placed it tenderly in the car and took it home. I did not know what I was going to do next. He had been a marvellous friend and I did not want to let him go. I was desperate to keep him and his memory alive. I even thought about getting him stuffed and wondered whether cloning could replace him. What I did not want to do was to burn his body.

The following day I left his body on the floor of the garage and drove down to the Surrey Pet Cemetery in South Godstone and bought a beautiful silk-lined wooden casket for £85.50. I decided against having him buried there, partly because of the cost but mainly because I wanted him to be buried at home in the garden.

When I returned home I was appalled to find that a few flies were already hovering around his body. Despite his body being stiff with rigour mortis I managed to fit him into an old fridge in the garage to help preserve his body. Following a conversation with my cousin Juliet, I realised that it would be a major task to bury the casket three or four feet deep in my own garden. As a result we decided that it would probably be better to bury him in a paddock close to his friend Conker the donkey.

On Thursday May 21st Ben took his final journey into the Surrey countryside accompanied by his casket which included some of his favourite toys: the Monkey, the Floppy Dog, the Scotty Dog and the tiny Teddy Bear, plus two plastic squeaky toys and a ball. To help him with his journey into the afterlife I enclosed a couple of well gnawed bones plus a

plastic envelope which contained a photograph of him and an account of his life, in case that his body was ever discovered at some time in the distant future.

As luck would have it, Juliet had access to a mechanical digger the following day and so Ben was buried in a beautiful place that he loved, beneath a small grove of trees, at the edge of a tiny paddock. When I saw how much earth that the digger had excavated I was glad that I had decided not to bury him in my small garden, as digging a three or four foot deep grave in London Clay, by hand, would have been a nigh on impossible task for me, who was told by my chiropractor when I first saw him in 1980, that I had the back of an old man. Forty-four years later I feel that I have grown into that back. The  accompanying photograph shows Juliet and her husband Bill filling in the grave watched by my cousin Carol, whilst the man with the old back supervised.

TIP NUMBER 15 - when burying a pet it is advisable to dig the grave at least three feet deep to protect the animal from burrowing predators. The grave should also be away from any water source that it might contaminate, and the pet should be buried in something bio-degradable if a casket is not used.

The simple grave was marked by a ring of stones surmounted by two small bunches of poinsettias. In my dreams I still like to think of Ben's spirit playing with Conker or chasing the rabbits which regularly grazed there every evening as the sun went down.

When I returned home my life seemed very empty and I felt extremely depressed. The window where Ben used to sit to watch the world go by was vacant and his bed in the kitchen was empty. Each morning when I woke up I expected to see him lying outside my bedroom door, but he was no longer there. It was hard to think that I would never see or hear my best friend again.

In an effort to cope with this loss I threw myself into my work and cricket, but my depression was not really helped by the number of messages of sympathy that I received from family and friends. They merely reminded me of what I had lost. There was even a hand written message the following week from Nick Dodds, the vet, when he had returned from holiday which simply said:

" I am very sorry that Ben was put to sleep last week. Unfortunately it was the kindest thing to do to prevent him suffering.

I hope to see you again under happier circumstances."

Although Nick must have experienced the death of an animal hundreds of times before, I think that he felt a special bond with Ben as he had treated him for over sixteen years. Perhaps the sense of sadness that he felt was the reason that no bill was ever sent to me for that final appointment with death.

As a life long hoarder I still have many of the letters that were written to me by friends in the eighties and nineties. Most of them were addressed to 'David and Ben'. There was even an invite for us both to attend a barbeque. To most people we were an inseparable couple.

As part of my coping mechanism with his death I was determined that I would never forget him. With that intention in mind I took some photographs of him to a local artist in Worcester Park, Pat Rhodes, who specialised in animal photographs. She produced this beautiful acrylic painting of Ben for a modest fee. I had it expertly framed and placed it in a prominent position in my bedroom. The disc on his collar simply says 'Ben'.

All the photographs of Ben that I had taken throughout his lifetime, no matter how poor, were gathered together and placed in an album whilst one of the photos was cut to size and ended up, with a lock of his hair, in a small gold locket, which I wore around my neck for several months until the period of mourning was over and new dogs arrived.

The extent to which Ben's death affected my neighbours astounded me. Most of them either sent sympathy cards or spoke to me in passing and expressed their condolences.

The most touching tribute, however, came from a lovely young sixteen year old girl, Joanne Greenoak, who lived next door but one. We regularly used to chat to each other whenever she passed the end of my drive and she always made a fuss of Ben. It came as a bit of a surprise to me when she asked if she could have a photograph of Ben as she wanted to draw a picture of him.

A few days later she produced the accompanying portrait which compared favourably with that produced by the professional artist. Both artists faithfully captured the slight kink in the white blaze which ran from the muzzle to the forehead. Pat presented Ben with a quizzical look upon his face, whilst Joanne gave him a more solemn demeanour. I think I prefer Joanne's portrait as that was actually done from her love of Ben, the dog.

A copy of a letter that I sent to Nick Dodds on June 8th showed that I was resigned to Ben's death and thinking of finding a possible replacement. My letter also revealed that the small friendly veterinary practice had been taken over by a much larger organisation, the Wingrave.

"Thankyou for your letter of condolence about Ben's sad death. It was a blow at the time but in a way it was not really all that unexpected. His health had always been delicate and I am sure that he would not have lived half as long without your kind professional attention. It is comforting to know that he had a happy, contented life and was loved by nearly everyone who met him. It will be difficult to replace him but I have already begun the search. There is no doubt that I will make him a patient of the Wingrave although I hope that he will not have to attend so often."

It was probably a sign of my desperation to rekindle the spirit of Ben that I totally ignored Tip Number 1 about making sure that one bought a new puppy from a reputable source. Ben was such a brilliant dog that I felt that if I returned to the place from whence he came, I might be lucky enough to obtain a carbon copy of my beloved friend. It was a futile dream, as now, after forty years as a Border Collie lover, I am fully aware that no two dogs are the same and that is what makes them so interesting.

In the hope that I might be able to find a dog with all the wonderful qualities which Ben had possessed I rang up the Cottage Kennels in Cardigan, who at first seemed very reluctant to talk to me, but eventually they told me that they hoped to be sending a new litter to Petsville in late July.

The constant animal rights' protests outside the beleaguered pet-shop did not deter me from my aim of buying another Ben. I snuck in and put a deposit down on a male Border Collie puppy that I hoped would arrive in a few weeks time.

I was obviously not worried at the time that I might be buying a dog with all the health problems that Ben had suffered. I have to admit that what I ended up with in July was not what I anticipated.

Whilst I waited, much of my time was spent visiting Ben's grave and my newly found family in Ewhurst and their wonderful, photogenic dogs such as Penny.

Benji & Gemma - Double Trouble

Life has a knack of not turning out how one would like it to turn out. On Thursday July 23rd, 1998 I received a phone call from Petsville to say that the puppies that they were expecting from Wales would no longer be coming to their Sutton store, but would be arriving at their Kingston branch the following day and, if I were still interested in acquiring the dog, I would have to travel to Kingston to collect him.

Early the following Monday morning I braved the one-way system in Kingston and, after several wrong turns, managed to find the Petsville store at 68, Richmond Road. At the back of the shop was a small cage which housed three tiny nine week old Border Collies, two girls and a boy. They were all that were left of a much larger litter that had been born on May 22nd in Cardigan.

One of the bitches, with a distinctive diamond shaped patch of white fur on her forehead, seemed much livelier than the other two puppies and immediately attracted my attention. It was then that I made the impulsive decision that I would buy her as well as the boy, so that they would be company for each other. It was not a cheap decision as each dog cost me £179, plus £24 for the vaccination that they had received at the Manor Clinic the previous Friday, plus £34.51 V.A.T. for a grand total of £237.51 each. With all the dog food and other bits and pieces there was no change from £500.

Although buying dogs from a pet shop is usually frowned upon, I was quite impressed by the information provided by Petsville International upon how to look after a new puppy. For breakfast they recommended Warm Lactol with scrambled eggs; for lunch they suggested Eukanuba mixed with Denes Puppy food: whilst for dinner the dogs could be given boiled mince chicken and Eukanuba Puppy food. Even more impressive was the fact that they recommended that a new puppy should be registered with a vet within 48 hours of purchase and, if any serious medical condition were discovered, they guaranteed to return the full purchase price.

The dogs were placed in a box upon the back seat of my Nissan Micra and I eagerly drove them to their new home in Netley Close where I had already prepared the floor of the conservatory for their arrival with plastic sheeting and piles of old newspapers.

The photograph on the right is taken from a video of them that I made shortly after their arrival. They slept quite a lot and when they were not sleeping the bamboo furniture was ideal for chewing unfortunately.

I decided to call the bitch Gemma as a diamond is a gem, and the patch of white fur on her forehead almost resembled a diamond in shape. Gemma was also the name of a girl at Stanley Park who was the bane of my life, and it touched my sense of humour to think that whenever she annoyed me in the

future I would think to myself, "I named my dog after you."

As for the boy I really wanted to call him Ben in the hope that he would revive the spirit of my beloved friend. I eventually rejected that name as I felt that it made me appear rather pathetic, and so I decided to call him Benji or Ben junior, or just Junior.

Both these grainy photographs were taken from the video of their first outing into the garden, and despite the poor quality of the pictures their cute pink noses are just about visible. It became apparent when I watched the video that I had settled upon calling the boy 'Benji'.

The dogs were registered with the vet as soon as we reached home, and they had their first meeting with Nick Dodd the following day. He treated them both for fleas and gave Benji a little something for his dodgy tummy, plus advice to feed him upon something bland such as fish or chicken and rice.

The photograph on the right shows Benji, who was a reluctant eater, seemingly tucking into a bowl of his food.

I had been told, probably by the pet shop, that a puppy was less likely to be sick if it ate from a raised dish rather than from one on the ground. As a result I had bought an adjustable plastic frame from the pet shop that I screwed on to the garden shed. A

couple of silver dishes were attached to this frame by plastic catches, which allowed them to be moved to different heights depending upon the size of the dogs.

Benji's bland food was always placed in the left hand dish, whilst Gemma was supposed to have a mixture of Eukanuba puppy biscuits and Hills Diet Growth in the right hand bowl.

It might seem rather stupid that I fed both dogs at once, but it was the only way that I could encourage Benji to eat. Gemma, who was already larger than Benji, as can be seen in the adjoining photograph, had a great appetite and, of course, helped herself to the chicken and rice as well as her own food. But at least Benji did eat a little.

The adjustable feeding stand was quite a good idea but it did not last very long, as the plastic catches upon the bowls were eminently chewable for a couple of young puppies, as was the plastic frame itself. Although the frame ended up in a landfill, the bowls, with their chewed red catches, are still being used twenty five years later.

Life in the Garden and Conservatory

I am really pleased that I had the foresight to make a short film of the puppies' first couple of weeks with me before we were able to venture into the park. Being a teacher and being blessed with six weeks' summer holiday, I spent much of my time with Benji and Gemma in either the garden or the conservatory observing their behaviour and their reaction to a whole new world. The video reminds me of that wonderful time. In a way the pleasure that I felt from watching Benji and Gemma partially deadened my sense of loss from the death of Ben.

To the puppies the garden must have seemed enormous although in reality it is only about 120 square yards in area. Most of that was devoted to a poorly kept lawn, down the centre of which a path led to a hedge of five leylandii trees which overhung some shrubby vegetation in which a small dog could hide.

There were also plenty of items to chew whether it was a bone, a squeaky rubber toy, or in the case of the photograph on the right a piece of metal encased in concrete which had been the post hole for a washing line. Benji also made a rather futile attempt to try and grab a sheet which was hanging from the washing line.

The video reveals that from the very first day I made an initial start to train them to respond to my whistle. Whilst they were chewing the post hole I gave a very high pitched whistle. It took a couple of blasts before I really got a reaction. Benji looked up at me and I patted my knees and said, "Good boy!" He quickly worked out what I wanted and waddled over wagging his tail. After another blast his sister followed.

I also made a great fuss of the dogs whenever they weed or poo-ed in the garden. The adjoining photograph shows Benji squatting to wee on that first day, listening to me praise him. It took him several months to learn how to cock his leg. Within a fortnight he managed occasionally not to wee inside the conservatory. It took a little while longer to completely house train him.

TIP NUMBER 16 - heap plenty of praise upon ones puppy when it urinates or defecates in the garden.

As to pooing Benji liked his privacy, and from that first day he always hid behind one of the trees whenever he wanted to poo. Gemma was not quite as shy, and happily went upon the lawn, which was slightly easier to clear up.

Much of the puppies' time was spent play-fighting, which was sometimes quite worrying to watch as their little teeth were very sharp. They would roll around in a ball of fur for about ninety seconds growling, snarling and occasionally squealing, trying to grab each others' legs, ears or throats, before collapsing exhausted from their exertions. The accompanying photograph shows one of these battles; each dog trying to grab the other's legs. Fortunately the only real damage done was to their collars.

Danger in the garden

Benji's upset tummy could possibly have been the result of negligence upon my part as, the first time that I let them into the garden they seemed to make a bee-line for the sticks of rhubarb which were the only plants growing there. As soon as I saw them begin to nibble the large leaves, I scooped them both up in my arms and placed them in the conservatory whilst I stripped the rhubarb bed of all its plants.

TIP NUMBER 17 - do not let dogs eat rhubarb leaves as they contain high levels of oxalic acid, which is toxic to animals and can cause sickness, diarrhoea and difficulty breathing.

By removing the rhubarb I thought that the garden was a much safer environment for them to roam around. Little did I suspect that within four days both of them would spend several hours in the veterinarian hospital on a saline drip for suspected poisoning.

Like an idiot I had been working around the garden and had left the shed door open. Imagine my horror when I returned to the shed and found a packet of weed-killer had been ripped open in my absence. I rushed them both to the vets where they were both placed on drips for suspected poisoning, whilst I had to spend several hours at home waiting for the news that I had managed to kill both my wonderful little charges within the space of a week.

TIP NUMBER 18 - garden sheds often contain a variety of dangerous items which range from sharp implements to slug pellets, all which can prove fatal to a young puppy.

Although Benji and Gemma were returned to me that evening with a clean bill of health, a possible poisoning was not the only threat to their health that I encountered that week. A few days after I had bought them both metal disc name tags to attach to their collars, I found one of the badly chewed collars lying upon the ground with the name tag missing. A scan of the garden with a metal detector failed to reveal the tag as did a scan of both dogs. For the next day or two I had the rather unpleasant task of making a detailed search of all their poo, which fortunately revealed nothing of interest.

One danger which it was totally impossible to control was that posed by the urban fox. Every week letters appeared in the local press blaming foxes for the disappearance of beloved moggies. After watching our local foxes pass within a couple of yards of Oscar, the next door cat, and seen the indifference which they obviously felt towards one another, I found it hard to believe that foxes posed any threat towards a cat. As several of our neighbours regularly left food out for the foxes they had virtually become semi-domesticated.

Although I rarely saw foxes in my garden during the day time, it was obvious that they were regular night-time visitors as many of the dogs' toys which were left on the lawn would disappear overnight and end up next door in Geoff's garden.

Despite not believing that foxes regularly killed local cats, I was still slightly worried as to what might happen if a fox came across the puppies, who looked so small and vulnerable. Almost as worrying, however, was the fear that they might contract some disease such as roundworm, hookworm, lungworm, heartworm, tapeworm, listeria or salmonella from eating fox poo, or that they could become infected by fleas or ticks from being in close proximity to a fox. Mange was another terrible disease which could also be transferred to them via fox mites.

Tentative Training

Apart from getting the puppies to react to a whistle, towards the end of the first fortnight I decided to try them both on a lead with limited success. Benji did not appear to mind having the lead attached to his collar although he seemed to think that it was a game of 'tug', as he gripped the lead with his mouth and shook it all around as he walked along.

Gemma, on the other hand, for the first few occasions refused to stand when the lead was placed upon her. When eventually she was coaxed into taking a few steps, her performance was ruined by Benji jumping on her, grabbing the lead and pulling it as hard as he could.

I had been warned upon more than one occasion about the dangers of acquiring 'littermates', as it was widely believed that puppies from the same litter were more difficult to train, might struggle to socialise with other dogs and were more likely to bond with each other rather than with their owner. It was also recommended that one trained them separately, which I failed to do. I have got to admit that Benji and Gemma were not the best trained dogs but they were an endless source of fascination as there was definitely a strong telepathic bond between them, which often led to them demonstrating behaviour which one associates more with humans than with dogs.

I must also admit that I found the first two or three months very hard work, particularly trying to house train them. I was lucky, however, to have a conservatory with a concrete floor and a copious supply of clean newspapers. I think, however, that they did bond with me, or was it that I bonded with them? In a way, though, it was lucky that I had bought them in the summer holidays and could spend much of my time with them.

TIP NUMBER 19 - it is advisable not to buy puppies from the same litter unless one can devote a lot of time to them. They are more than double the trouble but twice the joy.

A couple of weeks later, the puppies having had their final vaccination shots, both ventured into the park, pulling on their extendable leads. I had obviously failed to teach them to walk to heel as they both shot ahead of me, each one wanting to be the leader of the pack. I must admit that this trend lasted for several years until they were quite elderly, despite the fact that I tried a variety of devices such as a choke chain and halties. I did not use the choke chain for long as I felt that it was cruel.

For the first few visits to the park I kept Gemma on an extendable lead and let Benji run free. There was absolutely no problem with him wandering off as he seemed more interested in attacking his sister than running away and came whenever I whistled. Within a week both the dogs were running free, chasing a ball and returning it to me.

One of their first encounters with another dog occurred at the end of August when we travelled to visit my cousin Juliet and her terrier Tiny at Forest Green. The photograph on the right shows how much the dogs had grown in the space of five weeks. They were obviously highly suspicious of Tiny.

As they seemed rather scared of other dogs, I decided that it would probably be advisable to book them onto a puppy training course so they could socialise: and so, in October 1998, I enrolled them both on a five week puppy training course with the Woodmansterne Dog Training Club, which met at the Diamond Riding Centre in Carshalton on Monday evenings. Although the riding centre was well lit, the evenings were often cold and miserable and my charges showed little improvement.

We had to do all the basic commands such as 'sit', 'stay', 'lie down' and 'walk to heel'. I think that I was the only one there trying to cope with two dogs. If I tied one of the dogs to a fence it would bark frantically, annoying everyone, and so I tried to train both dogs together. On the final week I was struggling so much to get Benji to walk to heel that the instructor, a police-dog handler, decided to show me how to do it. As it was obvious that Benji was not going to comply with his instructions, he passed the lead back to me within ten seconds. The puppy training experiment was basically a failure but at least Benji and Gemma did get to meet some other dogs.

Travelling by Car

For the first couple of years Benji suffered from acute car sickness which could be triggered by even a short journey to the vets, and so I had to make sure that he had not eaten anything for at least two hours before making a journey. Gemma, however, was fine but, as they both travelled on the back seat of the Micra, her brother being sick did affect her.

I remember on one occasion, as I drove along, being alerted by the sound of Benji being sick. Briefly turning around I saw that the back seat was swimming in his regurgitated breakfast, whilst Gemma, in her turn, was standing upon her hind legs with her paws over the back seat trying to avoid the mess. It was almost as though she was saying, "Please let me out of here!"

The Dog Flap

About a month after acquiring the new puppies I made a stress saving investment thanks to Malcolm Evans, one of my cricketing friends, who apart from being a qualified electrician was a jack-of-all-trades. One day when he had come round to the house to fit a new oven he saw that I was still struggling with the house training, and so he suggested that he could knock a hole in the wall of the conservatory and fit a dog flap.

Although I was a little bit wary of having an electrician let loose upon the brickwork with a hammer and chisel, I decided to go ahead with the scheme. I bought a dog flap from the local pet shop in Worcester Park and within 24 hours Malcolm had done a magnificent job. He had even built a step outside the conservatory to aid their access.

There was absolutely no problem in getting Benji to use the dog flap. I showed him how to use it once and after that he was happy to use it whenever he wanted to go into the garden. He was a very bright boy who was always eager to please. His sister was another story. I literally had to push her through the flap for about six weeks before she would use it by herself.

The photograph on the right shows Benji making a slow entrance into the extremely untidy conservatory that was their home. In the centre of the room was a large, tatty green carpet which the dogs were forever trying to turn upside down, whilst around the perimeter was a layer of newspapers which were kept in place by strategically placed bricks. This was where the dogs had been encouraged to wee before the flap was built, and on the shelves surrounding the conservatory were stored piles of old newspapers.

For almost a year the conservatory was in a constant state of chaos as can be seen in the photograph on the left where at least nine bricks, an old mangle, a small shed and a dustbin were employed to keep the newspapers and the carpet in place. Even the dogs' water bowl outside had a brick in it as Benji seemed to take great delight in knocking it over.

It took almost until the end of 1999 before the conservatory was fit for human habitation. All the newspapers were removed, the walls were repainted, the floor was carpet tiled and radiators were installed. In a way the room was transformed into a rather luxurious kennel, although a few bricks were still strategically placed at weak points in the defences, and the small shed became a store cupboard for all their bits and pieces.

By the turn of the millennium the dogs were much larger as can be seen from the photograph of Gemma standing on the step outside the dog-flap. Her body almost seemed to fill the aperture.

The dog-flap was a great boon in that the dogs could let themselves into the garden if they needed to go to the toilet. I also managed to position the security light upon the wall into such a position whereby, if any animal stood upon the step, half the garden and the conservatory would be bathed in light for about five minutes. That was very useful in allowing one to keep watch upon what the dogs were doing from the kitchen.

I have always found, however, that if you solve one problem with a dog another problem is sure to emerge. In this case instant access to the garden also meant that they could indulge in midnight barking to really annoy the neighbours.

To curb this problem, and at great expense, I bought a couple of aboistop collars and a handful of citronella aerosol cans from the Petsville pet shop. Basically there was a small white box upon a collar into which one could squirt citronella. The device was battery operated and fired a jet of the extremely unpleasant vapour if ever the dog barked. It did modify Gemma's behaviour more than Benji's. On occasions it almost seemed as though he was demonstrating what a macho dog he was, and he wore the smell of citronella as though it was a badge of honour. He was obviously unaware how expensive each refill was!

In order to cope with Gemma's first (and last) season in mid-1999, I bought a couple of cages that I placed in both the living room and the conservatory to keep the dogs apart. As an added precaution Benji was looked after for about a week by an elderly friend, Renee Steel, who lived on the Malden Road. He did blot his copybook on one occasion, when she took him a walk in the park, by running home.

Gemma's season, therefore, was less of a problem than I imagined that it would be and, shortly thereafter, both cages were placed next to each other in the conservatory. Fleeces lined the bottom of the cages, blankets covered the roof and sides and the

doors were usually unlocked. They were quiet, safe spaces where the dogs could sleep at night, or where they could rest during the day time. Gemma, being the dominant dog, took the cage next to the radiator.

Although I tried to stop him at first, Benji took a great delight

in chewing his fleece, which eventually, after several years, had hundreds of small holes in it and became known as 'Your Chew'. To him it was a security blanket, and as such I did not have the heart to throw it out, although by the end of his life it was almost more hole than blanket. He would lie there for hours on end, holding the fleece with his paws, gently chewing as though he were deep in thought.

One side effect of this constant chewing, however, could have been the reason that his teeth were in a much better condition than those of his sister, who had to be operated upon twice to clean her teeth. Did Benji's constant chewing of his fleece keep his teeth clean?

Three night time incidents occurred during the first few years of Benji and Gemma's life with me, which vividly remain in my memory. The first occurred on New Year's Eve, 1999. Being an extremely boring, antisocial creature I had decided to spend the evening alone with the dogs, quietly making one or two phone calls and watching television. I really was not too impressed by all the hype about the new millennium.

I let the dogs into the garden, at what I thought was about 11.50, so that they could go to the toilet before they retired. All was very quiet, and from the light of the security lamp I watched them wander around the garden. Sadly I had mis-judged the time by several minutes as suddenly all hell was let loose as rockets, flares and explosions seemed to erupt all around us. The dogs shot into the conservatory with their tails between their legs, and I followed closely behind them. They were noticeably more scared of fireworks following this experience that they had been before.

Terror in the Night (1)

On the whole the dogs were relatively quiet and spent most of their nights inside their cages. This was not the case a couple of years later when I was awoken at about three o'clock by a cacophony of barking. I wearily staggered to the side window and shouted at them to be quiet, but to no avail. It sounded as though they were fighting. As a lodger was in the down-stair's bedroom I had to stagger down a couple of flights of stairs and out of the front door of the house into the porch in my pyjamas.

I exited the porch and rounded the corner of the house and stood there looking over the gate into blackness as the security light had gone off, as the dogs had been outside barking for over five minutes. It sounded as though they were within about twenty feet of me, fighting, squealing and barking in the narrow passageway at the side of the house. I bellowed at them to be silent, and for a split second silence ensued, before a dark shape with glaring eyes launched itself over the four foot six inch tall gate, knocking me to the ground.

I was rather stunned for a moment and then rose to my feet, opened the gate and checked that both dogs were alright when the security light came on. I noticed a little blood on my hand which I hoped was not a bite, but was the result of it being scraped on the wall as I fell. The following day I also noticed a trace of blood on the top of the gate which had presumably been left by my assailant. Although no damage appeared to have been done to the dogs, for over a year I suffered from a recurring nightmare, where a dark shape with glowing eyes threw itself at my head, and then was gone.

The culprit could have been the character on the right, whom I photographed, at about that time, lying upon the roof of the shed next door, camouflaged by some overhanging foliage.

Terror in the Night (2)

On another occasion I took the dogs downstairs so that they could go to the toilet before going to bed. I watched as they went into the garden, before turning to go to bed myself. As I closed the door I heard a horrible, blood-curling howl of pain. The security light was still on but I could not see the dogs who had disappeared beyond the leylandii.

I unlocked the door of the conservatory and made my way across the lawn and through the trees towards a chain link fence at the end of my property from where the howling emanated. It was difficult to make anything out as the light went off, but using a sense of feel I realised that Benji's head was trapped by the fence.

As I felt around his head, and as he tried to snap at me, I came to the horrifying realisation that a hooked strand of the fence had entered his eye. I just did not know what to do! I could not leave him there whilst I went to find a torch as he was in a lot of pain. And yet, what if I pulled his eye out?

I gritted my teeth and whispered comforting words to him before pushing the wire downwards and away from him. It came loose and he ran back towards the house. I caught up with him and expected to see an empty eye socket. Much to my relief the wire had obviously gone under the eyelid, hooking him like a four legged fish.

Although the eye was bloodshot and there was blood around the eyelid, he did not appear to be overly damaged, and, thanks to a course of anti-biotics he made a complete recovery. The chain linked fence, however, was dismantled the following day, and was eventually replaced by a wooden fence complete with prickle strips to discourage cats, foxes and possibly undesirable humans climbing over the fence.

TIP NUMBER 20 - remove any damaged chain linked fencing or any low level branches on trees as they could seriously damage a dog's eyes.

Benji and Gemma - two contrasting characters - one great team

From their very first week in Netley Close it was very evident that I had acquired two dogs with totally different characters. Gemma was the more dominant and needy of the siblings and tended to push her smaller brother around. She was also more confident in reacting with me and was forever pawing me for attention. Benji was quieter and more laid back, but I quickly found out that he was much more intelligent. He also displayed several of the emotions and character traits that one tends to associate with humans, such as intelligence, frustration, anger, love, empathy for others and probably most surprisingly - a sense of humour.

Gemma was a slow learner as was exemplified by her seeming inability to use the dog flap. A sadder illustration that she had a learning problem was her inability to catch a gently lobbed tennis ball. I know that I was a Special Needs teacher when I acquired the dogs, but I never thought that I would acquire a Special Needs dog. When I lobbed the ball Gemma would rise upon her hind legs and try to catch the ball in her front paws. It took several days for her to master using her mouth to catch a ball despite watching her brother's amazing eye/mouth dexterity.

Although Gemma seemed, to a large extent, to crave my attention, she did have a definite streak of independence and often ventured much further away from me than her brother. She loved to scatter the flocks of seagulls on the Rec. and would often chase them solo until she was a dot on the horizon, but she always returned at the sound of my whistle.

For the first eighteen months poor Benji found himself being bullied both physically and mentally by his larger sister. Physical bullying, such as pushing him aside when eating, was easy to see but the mental bullying surprised me. On one occasion I remember sitting on the L-shaped settee watching television with Gemma on the right hand side and Benji on the left. At one point Gemma turned and stared at him. Benji immediately got off the settee and walked over to the corner of the room and sat there for several minutes just staring at the wall as though he were being punished. There was obviously an extremely strong telepathic link between the pair.

When they were eighteen months old an event occurred which saw the bully being overthrown. I was taking them into the house along the corridor which led to the foot of the stairs when Benji suddenly attacked his sister, for reason unknown, and threw her to the floor with his teeth around her throat. She screamed in terror and I dragged him off. He had not bitten her but she was terrified of him and for several days refused to walk past him in the corridor unless I was there to make sure that she was safe. After that Gemma did seem to treat her brother with a little more respect and they settled into quite a loving relationship.

Benji, in his turn, was very protective of Gemma and sympathetic to her feelings. On one occasion we were walking in the park with two or three friends who all had dogs. One of these dogs was making amorous advances towards Gemma and it was obvious that she felt uncomfortable. Benji, sensing his sister's distress, continually placed himself between the amorous dog and his sister and successfully shielded her from the unwanted attention.

It was a few years later that I really recognised how intelligent Benji was. On the surface he appeared to be a gentle, friendly laid back dog whose idea of bliss was to sleep on his back with his paws in the air, clutching one of his toys. Beneath that laid back exterior, however, lurked a surprising comprehension of the spoken word.

On one occasion I was at the bottom of the stairs searching for my keys as I was about to go out, whilst Benji lay at the top of the stairs watching me with apparent disinterest. I could not find my keys and cried out to no-one in particular, "Where are my keys?" Benji immediately stood up, raised himself upon his rear legs and stamped down upon the top step three or four times. I immediately went upstairs and found the keys were next to him. I was flabbergasted as I had never tried to teach Benji the word 'key'. He obviously understood a lot more than I gave him credit for.

Another example of his understanding of the spoken word and his caring nature, occurred several years later when I discovered a baby dunnock or robin, which could not fly, hopping around the garden (see photograph on the right). I was worried that the tiny bird would fall prey to a passing cat or some other predator. As Benji seemed fascinated by the tiny bird, and as I had to go out for the rest of the day, I told him to keep an eye upon her. My last sight of the bird that day was of her being followed around the garden by a large gentle dog. What was even more surprising was the sight of him still following her around the following day, walking about a yard behind her with his nose to the ground.

Another indication of Benji's intelligence and his understanding of the spatial environment was that he occasionally resorted to deception and detour behaviour. If, for example, there was something on the lawn that he wanted, but was forbidden to have, he would pretend that he was not interested. He would casually wander around the garden and approach the object from another direction, hoping perhaps that I had not noticed.

The best example of this behaviour occurred on an occasion when I decided to try metal detecting in a large paddock that belonged to my cousin Juliet. I had decided to allow the dogs the freedom to explore the large field in the centre of which stood two lovely docile horses grazing. It was Benji's first sight of a horse and he decided to attack and started to run towards the horses. I immediately yelled at him and he came to a halt and started to walk with Gemma around the extremity of the field.

Benji had not forgotten what he wanted to do, however, and when he reached the other side of the field he attacked again before I could stop him. It could have been very serious but on this occasion it was quite amusing. The horse seemed unperturbed and gazed nonchalantly at him. Benji in his turn looked up at the horse which loomed over him. With a large dog he would have seized it by the neck and thrown it to the ground but as he stared up at the figure towering over him he took the only reasonable course of action. He turned around and walked away.

Frustration and Anger

This photograph shows the two young dogs playing with a blue plastic cube in the conservatory. The cube has a hole in the centre into which one can place small biscuits. If one can turn it upside down one might get a treat.

Several years later I re-introduced the cube to the dogs in the living room, and lived to regret it. Benji became more and more

frustrated with the cube as he could hear the biscuits rattling around inside it. He would growl at Gemma if she came near him and bashed the cube around so violently with his nose and paws that he was in danger of damaging either himself or the furniture. The cube was supposed to stimulate a dog's intelligence, but in Benji's case it made a normally very placid dog extremely angry. I gave the dogs a treat and removed the source of Benji's anger. A soft squeaky toy or bone was much better for his sanity.

Benji's Wicked Sense of Humour

A sense of humour is not a trait that most people would associate with a dog, but one incident which involved Benji seemed to suggest otherwise.

It was late one evening, the dogs were in the conservatory, and it was raining extremely heavily when I heard Gemma barking outside. I went to the window and noticed that the security light had been activated. I was mystified as to what the stupid dog was doing outside and so I quickly went downstairs.

As I entered the conservatory I was met by the loud drumming of the heavy rain as it hammered down upon the triple layered plastic roof, and there sitting with his back to the dog-flap was Benji. I shouted at him to move and, as he walked away, he threw his head back with his mouth wide open, in what can only be described as silent laughter. Gemma, who was soaked to the skin, came in and shook herself, spraying

water all over the place. She then walked over to Benji and for a good couple of minutes stood in front of him, continually poking him in the face with her pointy snout as though to say, 'I did not find that very funny!'

Team Work

It became obvious from our first outing on the Rec. with a ball that the dogs worked as a team. I would throw the ball and Benji usually caught it and dropped it for Gemma to return it to me. When I used a ball on a rope their team-work was even

more pronounced. They would run around me in a clockwise direction waiting for me to throw the ball. I usually aimed the throw towards Benji who would be about 50 yards away from me with his sister running slightly closer to me. Sometimes he would catch the ball on the full and sometimes after it had

bounced once. He would run on with it for about 20 yards before dropping it for his sister who probably felt that she had the more important role of returning it to me. We would keep that sequence up for about ten minutes. By that time the dogs had probably covered a couple of miles. It was a great way to exercise the dogs if one did not have enough time for a long walk, and it was probably why a veterinarian report upon them when they were two years old commented upon how fit they both were.

Passers-by would stop and watch them in admiration and often asked how I had trained them to run around me in circles. My usual answer was that I had not trained them, but that they had trained me to throw a ball to them whilst they ran around.

On one occasion we were playing with the ball on a rope towards the top of the Rec. where the grass had been allowed to grow waist high for ecological reasons. The large arc of the circle that Benji transcribed around me passed through this long grass, which led to the amusing spectacle of Benji's head popping into the air every few yards as he ran through the long grass in order that he could check where I was standing.

On several occasions other dogs became excited at the sight of two dogs running past them and would try to join in the chase but they usually quickly fell by the wayside, or would be flattened by Benji who seemed to be oblivious to any obstacle in his path. There would usually be a squeal of pain from the other dog, whilst Benji would quickly get to his feet and carry on running. He was basically obsessed with his work.

When the ball was replaced with a frisbee the dogs continued to work in the same fashion, mainly because Gemma was not too adept at catching the rotating disc, whereas her brother made some spectacular grabs.

The photograph on the right is one of my favourite ones of the dogs and I have an enlarged copy of it in my living room. It was taken one very sunny December day on the Rec. in front of my house (on the left). It shows a very athletic Benji catching a frisbee that was over seven feet off the ground. Gemma was looking on in admiration at her flying brother, and one could almost see her wondering how he managed to jump so high.

A Walk in the Park

As a dog owner I feel quite privileged to live next to Cheam Rec., which is an area of open parkland to the north of Cheam Park. On the western border of Cheam Park and Cheam Rec., which totals 61 acres in area, is a narrow strip of woodland, beyond which lies the wonderful Nonsuch Park, where Henry VIII built a fine Palace in 1538. This park is a magnet for dog owners for miles around who, once they have exhausted all the paved and unpaved paths which meander through the 300 acres of Nonsuch Park, can venture into the adjoining 56 acres of Warren Farm which is managed by the Woodland Trust.

For the first year of Benji's and Gemma's lives I tended to limit our activities to the Cheam Park and Rec. area. Our runs in the morning were usually confined to the Rec., whilst if any shopping needed to be done in the Village, we tended to walk through Cheam Park rather than take the more direct route along the Malden Road. Walking through the Park the dogs could be let off the lead to chase a ball, which was easier than having them pull me along the main road.

When they were about fifteen months old I bumped into a lady called Bernie, whom I had walked with on several occasions when Ben was alive. Bernie had two charming dogs called Triff and Lady, who tolerated my lively youngsters. Bernie spent over an hour every morning walking her dogs across the Rec., through the woods, past the Mansion House and tea rooms, around the outskirts of Warren Farm, and back through Nonsuch Park to Netley Close.

The photograph on the right is the only one that I have of Bernie and was taken in about 2003 when Benji and Gemma accompanied me on a cricket tour to the Isle of Wight. By that stage Bernie had moved with her husband and mother to a beautiful house in Shanklin Old Village on the edge of the Downs. In the photograph she is sitting behind Lady on the left and Janni who had

replaced Triff. Bernie actually looked after my terrible twosome for a few hours that day whilst I went to play golf, despite the way that they had disgraced themselves four years earlier.

For a period of about two or three months in 1999 it became a regular habit to meet up with Bernie and her dogs at the gate to the Rec., and to accompany her on her walk. On several occasions we met up with other dog walkers, whom I was keen to impress with my beautiful, well trained animals. One of our regular partners in our slow meander around the park was a charming lady with three Border Collies.

All went well for the first few encounters and then for some unknown reason, signs of animosity occurred between one of her dogs and Gemma when we reached Warren Farm. Then the unthinkable happened! Her dog ran away, chased by Benji and Gemma!

No matter how loud we shouted, or I whistled, made any difference as the dogs disappeared in the distance. The owner of the other collie and I tried to run after the three dogs but they were soon out of sight. After an hour we decided that a further search of the park was pointless and that there was a chance that our dogs had returned to their respective homes.

When I returned to Netley Close there was no sign of either Benji or Gemma. Whilst I was debating whether to ring the police or the R.S.P.C.A. the telephone rang. It was the owner of the other Border Collie ringing to say that all three dogs had run over two kilometres past the site of Henry VIII's Palace, and then across the very busy A24, London Road, to her home in Stoneleigh, where one of her neighbours had slipped leads upon my dogs, who were waiting for me to collect them.

I was more than a little relieved to be able to drive and collect them, especially as I realised that they must have been very lucky to have survived crossing the A24. Needless to say we rarely ventured beyond the woods into Nonsuch Park for several years after that encounter, mainly because I was too embarrassed.

TIP NUMBER 21: Do not be complacent or overconfident that you have total control of a young Border Collie. Beneath that seemingly obedient façade there might lurk an animal who wants to break free of the shackles of human control.

Benji and Gemma - house dogs

Although Benji and Gemma spent much of their early life in the conservatory, the amount of time that they spent inside the house increased as they grew older and as I became more confident in their level of house training. They did, however, have a penchant for chewing things such as table legs, which kept me constantly on my toes. I made sure that there were plenty of bones and toys around that I encouraged them to chew. My main fear was that they might try to nibble one of the electric cables which strewed the living room floor. Thankfully none of my dogs have seemed remotely interested in trying to electrocute themselves.

I can remember clearly the first time that I switched on the television. They seemed amazed to see the moving figures and they both went behind the set to see if the small characters were there. When they discovered there was nothing there, they soon lost interest in the novelty. I did try to interest them in sheep dog trials, but failed. There was one television incident, however, which defied my understanding.

Gemma's 'Emmerdale Farm' phobia - in about 1971 I spent eleven weeks off work with a combination of glandular fever and yellow jaundice. During that time all I could really do was either read or watch television. It was then that I acquired a lifetime love of watching 'Emmerdale Farm' and 'Coronation Street'.

In Netley Close I would make my evening meal at about six o'clock, feed the dogs, let them into the garden for a few minutes, then lie on the settee in the lounge to watch 'Emmerdale' whilst the dogs usually lay by the window, either sleeping or watching passers-by. Suddenly one evening in about 2002 when the 'Emmerdale' theme tune wafted over the airwaves, Gemma jumped onto the cushion above my head. Half of her weight was on the cushion and the other half upon my head.

I obviously made her get down and she returned to the rug in front of the window. Twelve minutes later when the theme tune was repeated to herald in the adverts' break, she shot back on to the cushion. This behaviour was repeated every time that she heard the theme tune for several months until suddenly she stopped. I could not think of any incident which had occurred in her life which might have triggered this behaviour.

The rather insipid photograph on the right shows the extremely grotty settee upon which I used to lie to watch TV. It was also a favourite resting place for Gemma. Those cushions on the left are the ones upon which I used to rest my head.

It was at about the same time as the 'Emmerdale' phobia that I acquired another lodger, Lesley Mayer, who was an old girlfriend of my long-time lodger, Colin Ritchie. They had decided to rekindle their old romance and Lesley obtained a job at St. Helier Hospital working as a physiotherapist. She was another dog lover and got on extremely well with the terrible twosome. Her sister, who stayed with us for a few days, was a vet who had studied in South Africa with Johnny Kriek who was working at the Wingrave at that time and had treated both of my dogs. It is sometimes a small world.

Lesley was a breath of fresh air and the dogs loved her. Whilst Colin worked on his computer, or on his minis, or his vintage E-type Jaguar, Lesley would happily watch Buffy or the soaps with me. Colin did not have a very high opinion of such rubbish, but would be avidly glued to 'Top Gear', Formula1 races or James Bond films.

It was a sad day for the dogs and myself when the couple, and Sid the snake, had to move out and return to South Africa, as it was impossible for them to access the housing ladder in the U.K. But at least the trailer vanished from the drive.

As the mortgage had been paid off, there was no longer any need to look for another lodger to fill the gap left by Colin and Lesley. There was not a lot of room either as I am a hoarder. My father had died in 2004 and I ended up hiring a van to bring back to Cheam many of the items, ranging from personal letters and photographs to furniture, which I could not bear to part with. My mother had been an avid writer and much of her writing was based upon handed down family anecdotes that I hope one day to be able to turn into a book.

The only lodger that I had following Colin and Lesley was Roger Boothman, an old school friend from Nelson Grammar School, who needed somewhere to stay for about three months whilst he moved house. In 1975, as neither of us could afford to get on to the housing ladder separately, we bought a small two bedroom townhouse in South Sutton for about £13,000. I thought that it was a good idea at the time as we both played cricket for Worcester Park and occasionally partnered each other at bridge.

The partnership was dissolved the following year as our characters were like chalk and cheese. I was a dog lover, whilst he preferred cats. I bought him out and he had enough to buy a flat in Teddington. We still remained friends, however, and regularly played bridge together at Wimbledon B. C. and the Lensbury Club where I was the captain of the league team. Our greatest success occurred in about 1990 when we recorded a top ten finish in a European competition out of several thousand pairs.

Without lodgers life was much quieter in the house and I chose to stay at home in the evenings with my dogs rather than play bridge.. There were, however, occasionally visits from family members who might possibly stay for a day or two.

One of the most welcomed visitors to the house that the dogs saw almost every day was Michael Gray, the milkman. He always made a fuss of them, whilst they regularly greeted him by jumping onto his milk float, looking for a treat.

Benji and Gemma - Cricket Lovers

For over thirteen summers Benji and Gemma accompanied me to cricketing venues around the South of England. I can not honestly say that they loved cricket, but they certainly enjoyed meeting people and visiting a variety of grounds from Norfolk in the East to Cornwall in the West, and to the Isle of Wight in the South.

The photograph on the right shows them in a typical cricketing situation, being tethered to a fence or bench for about five hours nearly every Saturday and Sunday afternoon, and for occasional midweek games in the summer. As I usually batted number eleven, the dogs tended to have my company for a couple of hours whilst I scored. This photograph was probably taken on a Worcester Park cricket tour to either Devon or Dorset. Rob Waite and Joe Hill looked to be keeping their distance at the far end of the bench.

The most enjoyable time at a cricket match for the dogs was obviously after the match when they were allowed to run loose. The following photograph was taken from a video that I shot at Worcester Park when the dogs were fifteen months old in 1999.

We tended to return to the home ground after every game to socialise, and whilst I relaxed from the rigour of captaining the Third XI the dogs would join in a game of football with any of the youngsters who could always be found there kicking a ball

around. With their arrival the game usually developed into one of quickly passing the ball around to stop the dogs gaining control of the ball. It was a game that was definitely enjoyed by both the dogs and the youngsters and any watching parents.

There were definitely no complaints from the parents or the children about their behaviour, even when Benji in his enthusiasm to head a ball dived straight through the torso of a five year old who ended up flattened and in tears. Thankfully his father was watching and seemed to think that it was rather amusing.

Benji did blot his copybook on one occasion in 2001, however, when I was walking him through the crowded clubhouse on a lead. One of the other members was sitting there with a bulldog on his lap, and as we walked past, Benji turned his head and bit the bulldog once and walked on. I already knew that my dogs did not like Boxers, but did not realise that their dislike of Boxers stretched to Bulldogs as well. Although I could see no damage the owner made a song and dance about it and took his dog to the vets, for which I was billed over £70.

In about 2009 the unthinkable happened at the cricket club and all dogs were banned from the ground. I wrote a strong letter of complaint but to no avail as there was a very powerful, small vociferous anti-dog group who held a disproportionate amount of power at the club. I was really extremely annoyed and for two years I refused to even enter the ground, which in a way was quite awkward as I was a captain. It meant that I would only play away games where the dogs were welcome.

One of the reasons for the club's so-called decision to ban dogs was to stop nearby residents walking their dogs on the ground before they went to work, and failing to pick up any poo left by their animals. I find it rather ironic that although dogs are banned from the ground, it appears to be home for numerous foxes who leave their foul smelling excrement dotted all around the outfield. I even encountered one last year blithely coming out of the changing rooms.

What was really ironic was that Benji and Gemma were still welcomed at several prestigious clubs such as the Bank of England, Lensbury, Beddington and Banstead, plus all of the clubs in the Surrey Hills where we played most of our Sunday games, and yet they were banned from a club that they had attended for over ten years.

Benji and Gemma were very popular both with members of my own team and with most of our opponents as they regularly put on an exciting display of ball or frisbee catching after the game. There was generally no lack of volunteers to walk them around the outskirts of the ground whilst the match was in play, although the volunteers were often less happy to make use of a poo bag.

I still vividly remember walking the dogs around the boundary at Mynthurst on one occasion with James Cameron, a rather brash character who insisted upon being allowed to walk Benji. I led the way with Gemma, whilst Benji and James walked a couple of yards behind us. Benji was not happy with that arrangement and when he managed to get close enough he nipped the back of my leg to show his disgust with that arrangement. He was, after all, my dog and I should not forget it.

Cricket Tours

Benji and Gemma took part in several tours with Worcester Park Cricket Club in the first decade of the twenty-first century. Having dogs along rather restricted my participation in the social side of the tours. Late night clubbing and general drunken behaviour was out of the question as was early morning streaking through some unsuspecting market place. For myself and the dogs a tour meant plenty of walking through the countryside, with a game of cricket in the afternoon. Being a member of the National Trust, the R.S.P.B. and English Heritage also gave me an opportunity to take advantage of those memberships in several places.

The first tours that the dogs attended were those organised by a Worcester Park elder, Nick Kingan, to some of the grounds with which he was familiar from his days as a graduate at Cambridge University. From 2001 to 2003 we visited the pristine lawns of Clare College, Cambridge, before visiting the ancient cathedral city of Ely and the beautiful countryside around Wisbech and March.

Probably the most enjoyable tours for the dogs, however, occurred in 2004 and 2005 when we stayed on the top floor of the Brocas Guest House in Sandown on the Isle of Wight, which was within a stone's throw of the beach where they could run every morning and evening. It was also relatively close to the home of our old friend Bernie and her dogs in Shanklin. The photograph on the right shows the happy duo in front of the Bed and Breakfast in Sandown.

Although these tours were only supposed to last for four days I tended to stay a little longer as I fell in love with the natural beauty of the island and the range of historical buildings that it offered, from the Roman Villa at Brading to the mediaeval castle at Carisbrooke and to the naval gun emplacements at the Needles,

For the second of these tours we had the company of my brother Bill who had a rather inflamed looking scar on his thigh from an accident that he had had a few days earlier. Against my advice he allowed Benji to lick the wound, and much to my amazement it healed completely within a few days. This course of treatment is not without danger of further infection.

One of my favourite walks with the dogs on the island entailed a visit to the National Trust carpark near the Highdown Inn, Totland Bay. From the carpark we climbed up several hundred feet to the Tennyson Monument, before walking over two miles along the National Trust owned Downs to the Needles with the dogs running free. Although there were small groups of sheep dotted around I kept a close eye on my dogs, as any responsible dog owner should.

Benji and Gemma and the Worrying Sheep Incident

It was noticeable from a very early age that Benji and Gemma had a inbred interest in sheep. Whenever we drove through the countryside, they would sit up and look out of the window if there were any sheep in the nearby fields.

On tour the dogs were even able to get a closer look at the animals which generations  of their forebears had been bred to protect and control. I often wondered how they would react if ever they came into close contact with a sheep. I think the answer to that question was 'badly'.

Probably the most embarrassing sheep/dog incident happened upon one of our visits to the Needles. We had parked as usual near the Highdown Inn and walked the two miles to the Needles. The dogs had run freely as the sheep were in the distance. On the return trip, however, I noticed that the sheep had wandered much closer to the path across the Downs. In fact at least sixty sheep straddled both sides of the path.

As I did not want to risk my dogs attacking the sheep I put them both upon their leads and carried on along the path. Benji and Gemma seemed quite agitated and pulled forward. The sheep, however, which looked enormous, moved closer to the path from both sides. The dogs panicked even more and pulled forward even harder, barking and yelping as they went. The sheep, on the other hand, had formed into a solid phalanx about six bodies wide and eight deep and followed about ten yards behind us. They obviously recognised the fact that Benji and Gemma were supposed to be sheep dogs and must have thought that I was a shepherd.

I made a bee-line towards a gate in one of the fences on the Downs. The dogs by this stage were really panicking. They were barking even louder and pulling harder in a forward direction whilst the flock of sheep followed closely behind. On the other side of the fence was a group of laughing Japanese tourists who were filming my predicament, but at least one of them helped take my bag whilst I struggled to open the gate in order to escape with just the dogs.

What was really embarrassing about this incident was the fact that my Border Collies were apparently frightened of sheep. They were the ones being worried, not the sheep.

****

A less dangerous walk that we visited quite regularly was around the grounds of the old ruined English Heritage Georgian mansion at Appuldurcombe where the gardens had been sculpted by Capability Brown. One could also visit the Owl & Falconry Centre displays upon the same site.

Another of our favourite places to visit on the Isle of Wight was the English Heritage owned medieval castle at Carisbrooke where one could stroll around the grassed moat and outer defences of the castle, and then walk around the battlements inside the castle walls. That was admittedly just a little dangerous with two dogs on leads and a possible fall on both sides. The

photograph on the right shows the dogs lying on a bank outside the ruined walls, whilst I watched a jousting tournament taking place upon the ancient parade ground.

I also toured the island with the Surrey Senior Cricketers, and Benji and Gemma, on one memorable occasion in the early years of the twenty-first century. One morning when we were due to play against Shanklin I decided to visit Bernie and Lady. After a coffee we had a beautiful walk across the Downs and clifftops towards Luccombe Bay. Several hours later, however, when the Seniors were due to start the match against Shanklin, I discovered that I must have dropped my phone on our walk. I spent the rest of the day wandering over the fields behind Bernie's property and along the clifftop path searching for my mobile phone, which led to a lot of ribbing from my fellow players. That phone was never found.

From 2006 to 2008 the Worcester Park Cricket Tour took us to the wonderful county of Devon where we played cricket in such marvellous places as Exmouth, Tavistock. Bovey Tracey and Ottery St. Mary. Whilst the other tourists tended to hire rooms in the halls of residence at Exeter University, because of the dogs I had to find alternate accommodation at Higher Southbrook Farm on the outskirts of the

tiny village of Whimple which is situated about nine miles from Exeter.

Although the bedroom was quite luxurious and featured a four poster bed and the food was delicious, there was not much to do locally apart from walk, mainly along the narrow country lanes where it was impossible to let the dogs off their leads. At night time it was at least a mile to the nearest pub.

Although there was a special breed of sheep in an adjoining paddock, all Benji and Gemma did was stare. Memories of the Isle of Wight were probably still fresh in their

minds. The photograph on the left shows them sitting on a small bridge close to the farmhouse. What I think is impressive about the photograph is the fact that, although they still have their leads on, they were not tethered to anything. They were quite happy to sit there and watch me take photographs of them from another bridge about fifty yards away.

Benji and Gemma were definitely accepted by most of the players as an integral part of the touring party. In the photograph on the right they were waiting patiently in front of Rob Hill, James Cameron and Joe Hill for one of the matches to begin. Benji looks typically laid back resting upon someone's cricket shoes, whilst Gemma appeared poised for action.

Probably the last tour that we took was one to Dorset in 2009. That one was basically an extremely wet occasion with only a couple of matches being played. For me the most memorable event was being turned away from one of the clubs by an officious gentleman who informed me that dogs were not allowed at the ground. I told him that if that was the case then I did not want to play there, and left.

Benji and Gemma at Cuddington Golf Club

As the golf club is only a twelve minute drive away from Netley Close, the dogs quickly became used to regularly visiting the club, where their behaviour was exemplary. Although they were on longish leads I would relinquish my hold on them whenever I needed to take a shot and they would lie there patiently watching. The only time that I needed to take extra care was when the squirrels were particularly active in chasing each other around in the spring.

In the summer I tended to play with an old teaching colleague from Glastonbury High School, John Joseph Murtagh, a member of a famous cricketing family and a non-dog-lover. John, however, was definitely a fair weather golfer who would not play in either rain or in the winter months. For much of the time, therefore, I played with only the dogs for company and was generally known as that 'old bloke with the dogs'.

On one occasion our journey to the golf club was abruptly terminated by a freak road accident. I was driving a Hyundai Trajet people-carrier which I had modified by removing one of the seven seats, to take all my golfing and cricket equipment and the dogs. It was a late afternoon in September when I decided, on a whim, to play a few holes of golf. With the dogs safely ensconced at the rear of the car, I drove along the A217 to the large roundabout at the start of the mad mile. I waited there whilst two cars driving south from Sutton entered the roundabout. The second car was too close to the first one and unfortunately clipped it and caused it, unseen by me, to rotate 180 degrees. As a result when I drove past the roundabout, out of the corner of my eye I noticed a car travelling towards me the wrong way around the roundabout.

I tried to accelerate out of the oncoming car's path but failed. There was a resounding crash as the side panels of the car were rather damaged and my door would no longer open. Fortunately I was unhurt and the dogs were safe, despite the fact that I had been too lazy to attach their harnesses to the seatbelts, as they had been flung sideways rather than forwards.

In a rather ironic stroke of fate, the woman who had caused the accident was married to one of my former pupils at Glastonbury H.S., and I had to suffer the indignity of

him seeing me being breathalysed as a participant in a road accident. I did inform the officer that he would have had a better chance of getting a positive reading if I had been leaving the golf club.

After about an hour and a half of being stared at by passing motorists the Traject eventually limped home, where it stayed for several days until it was deemed a 'write-off' by the insurance company.

Benji's attitude to Golf Of all my Border Collies I consider Benji to have been the most intelligent. Although I love the game of golf, I think that it was a sign of his intelligence that he was the only one of my dogs to have turned his nose up at the chance of going for a walk around the golf course. Having traversed the course hundreds of times by the age of twelve he was obviously bored with the game. He clearly belonged to the Mark Twain school of thought and considered golf as being a good walk ruined.

In his later years it became more difficult to tempt him into the car if he knew that we were going to the golf club, and yet he would quite happily get into the car if I said that we were visiting Dawn or Juliet or even going to the shops or the vets. If he were already in the car when we arrived at the golf club he would show no desire to get out, and would stay there quite happily, with the windows open, whilst I walked Gemma.

Benji and Gemma - Car Travellers

Once I had come to grips with Benji's car sickness problem, the dogs soon became seasoned car travellers on the back seat of my rather tiny Micra Passion. Within a couple of years that car was traded in for a Renault Kangoo which was more spacious but not very appealing, as it was basically a van with sliding doors. It did, however, allow easy access for the dogs. The Kangoo in its turn gave way to the more attractive Hyundai Trajet, or 'tragic' as I usually referred to it after it was written off.

All these cars had the same features in common: the back seat was covered with rather grubby sheets; there was usually a supposedly non-spill bowl of water on the floor, plus a seat was removed to provide additional storage space as, it did not matter how large the car was, I always managed to fill every available nook and cranny. When going on cricket tours it was obviously necessary to take my large cricket bag; my golf clubs as one never knew when the opportunity to play would occur; my cases and then an array of items that I might need such as a radio, cameras and binoculars.

What surprised me most, however, was the amount of equipment that it was necessary to pack for two dogs if one were going away for a few days. I usually packed all the food that they required, their silver metal bowls, their brush and comb, their bedding, their toys and bones, a copious number of towels, any medicine that they were taking and probably most importantly the special two sided brush for removing all traces of hair from the carpets of rooms in which we had stayed.

Benji and Gemma's Visits to Lancashire

One of the longest and most boring journeys that we regularly made was the two hundred and fifty mile trek to visit my father in St. Annes and my brother in Darwen. The journey tended to take approximately six hours as I dislike, if possible, travelling by motorways.

The photograph on the right shows my father in probably their first Christmas visit to St.

Annes trying to train the dogs. For someone who professed not to care about dogs he certainly spent a lot of time with them.

The photograph on the left shows Benji and Gemma relaxing upon my father's much larger and better kept lawn. It was taken in 2005 six months after my father's death, and before we managed to sell the bungalow.

When the dogs first visited St. Annes in 1998, my grandmother had just celebrated her hundredth birthday, and was by that stage living in a care home about a mile away in Links Road. We would call on her nearly every day whenever we visited St. Annes, much to the joy of all the other residents, as they loved the dogs. Helena Naomi Stemp died eventually in 2000 and was buried at Cranleigh.

The dogs loved St. Annes as it meant plenty of walks along the beach towards Blackpool or through the sand dunes to Lytham. The bungalow was also used as a base for numerous journeys further afield to places such as the Lake District, Pendle Hill or Darwen Tower with my brother. We were not too welcomed in his home as his wife was still allergic to dogs. Her allergy led to a memorable incident in St. Annes.

The Incident of the stolen cheese

One afternoon Bill and June visited St. Annes and went shopping before they came to the bungalow. In order to help June's allergy the dogs were shut in the corridor outside the dining room where we all sat for over an hour, having a cup of tea and a bite to eat. The dogs must have become bored and decided to explore the bags of shopping that June had left in the corridor. It must have been a pleasant surprise for them to find two pounds of cheese wrapped in tissue paper and they scoffed the lot. Whilst we found it amusing at the time I was far from amused when I had to clear up all the white diarrhoea in the next 24 hours.

TIP NUMBER 22: Whilst small amounts of cheese can be used as treats or to hide tablets, your dog might struggle to process the lactose in cheese. Regular amounts of cheese can also lead to dermatitis, pancreatitis, inflammatory bowel disease and obesity.

The Incident of the Large Porcelain Pig

Every morning in St. Annes, after I had taken the dogs for a walk around the Royal Lytham Golf Course, we used to wander up St. Thomas's Road and over the hump-backed bridge to the newsagents/post office. Next door to this shop there was a butcher's shop. On the first morning of a new visit to see my father I noticed that the butcher's shop had acquired a large three foot tall porcelain pig, which was stationed on the boundary between the two shops.

Feeling slightly mischievous I decided to wind Benji up just to see what he would do. Foolishly I said, "Look at that dog, Benji." Unfortunately Benji was on an extendable lead that was not in a locked position. He shot forward and threw himself at the pig, his teeth going for its neck. Bang! The pig exploded into thousands of pieces and

Benji stood there shocked with a look of embarrassment upon his face, whilst two or three passers-by stood there laughing. Benji's sense of embarrassment was probably not as great as mine when I had to go into the butcher's shop to explain that my Border Collie had destroyed their porcelain pig. I did offer to pay for the damage but fortunately they refused my offer, although I did not explain that the whole incident was down to my own stupidity and that the dog was not to blame.

Benji and Gemma's Kennel Experience

At Christmas time 2002 I had been invited to help my brother Bill delivering fruit and vegetables from his mobile van in Darwen. Bill's own children had helped in previous years but by that stage, realising what a hard thankless job it was, they declined to help him. Basically it was an eighteen hour day which began at six o'clock loading the van and ended at midnight by cleaning the van out. In between it meant constantly clambering in and out of the van to deliver Christmas cheer to his regular customers. As thanks I got to sleep in a corridor in a sleeping bag.

As my father was too old to look after the dogs I placed them in kennels near Blackpool for five days. After they emerged I vowed that I would never put my dogs in kennels again as both had acquired coughs and had upset tummies. This photograph shows them in their prison cell.

They had, however, acquired a new ball game in clink which they demonstrated upon my father's large lawn. One would run with a tennis ball in his or her mouth and then drop it. The other dog would swoop in, pick the ball up, run a few yards, then drop it. This sequence was repeated time and time again. They no longer needed me to throw a ball for them.

Following my father's death in 2004 our number of trips north reduced dramatically. Although we could stay in my brother's house opposite Bold Venture Park in Darwen, the dogs were confined to one of the bedrooms because of June's allergy. Cleaning the dogs after a walk in the park was a nightmare. At home I could hose them down in the back garden, give them a good towelling and leave them to dry off completely in the conservatory. Bill's house had a tiny backyard with a bucket of water and a sponge. I then had to take them into the house through the front door into a small porch where I had to try to towel them dry.

In 2008 Bill and June acquired a Labrador which had been crossed with a Jack Russell. It looked like a black Labrador with very short legs as can be seen in the photograph on the previous page, which was taken in front of Bill's back gate in 2013. Bill acquired Nelson on the understanding that if June's allergy could not be cured then Nelson would be returned to its previous owner.

A course of allergy tablets had worked wonders for June but did not help Benji and

Gemma. They still had to be shut in the bedroom when they visited Darwen as Nelson proved to be quite territorial. The dogs were wary of each other when out for a walk but had to be separated inside the house.

Upon one of our visits to Darwen I took this rather charming photograph on the left of Bill's step-grandson (if there is such a thing) Jamie, relaxing

with Benji and Gemma. It was the first time that they had met and shows how relaxed the dogs were in the company of children, and how most youngsters sensed there was nothing to fear from the beautiful pair of Border Collies, although Benji did once upset a passing youngster when he suddenly licked his ice-cream cornet.

Benji and Gemma's Trip to the Alps

In 1973 I had taught Bridge at Night School for three terms at Sutton Common Girls School. I made a handful of good friends there, including Jolyon Crosthwaite who was the son of my stockbroker, who lived in Belmont. Jolyon did not enter his father's world of high finance but worked in the wine department at Harrods. Eventually he decided that he wanted to make his career in the world of wine and went to broaden his education in France. There he met a pretty Italian girl called Corinne whom he married and they settled down in Grenoble where Jolyon, who retained his love of wine, became a teacher of English to mature students.

I kept in touch with Jolyon and Corinne over the years and would meet up with them whenever they came to England. They invited me to visit them in France on numerous occasions and said that I could stay in the small chalet that they had bought in the Vercors. For years I used the dogs as an excuse not to visit them until eventually in 2008 I took the plunge and ordered European Passports for the dogs which, with all the necessary injections, cost me about £250 apiece. These EU passports were much more convenient and easier to obtain and use than the current post Brexit documents. The picture on the previous page was Gemma's passport photograph.

Two days after the cricket season had ended, on Tuesday September 30th, I strapped Benji and Gemma into the Hyundai Trajet which was full to the brim with whatever I thought that we would need for a short holiday. I booked a return date for Thursday October 23rd, as I thought that three weeks would be enough. The holiday, however, was that pleasant that I made sure that I left the return date open on all future trips. If the weather was fine and the holiday was enjoyable we could perhaps stay away for a couple of months; but if the weather was poor we might return after a fortnight. Nowadays, unfortunately, one of the adverse effects of Brexit is that one has to adhere to a specific date of return. (Benji's passport picture is on the right)

Over the following decade I visited Grenoble on three further occasions with my dogs and the holidays tended to follow the same format. We would drive down to Dover and board a ferry to Calais. It would then take about four days to reach our destination and about three days to return to the Opal Coast. Overall we would travel over two thousand miles at approximately thirty miles per hour. The average speed was somewhat reduced by my having to constantly pull into laybys, either to let much faster French drivers overtake me, or to check my maps. As I have an aversion to motorways we tended to pass through hundreds of small villages where the speed limit was often 20 or 30 kph. My main aim, in which I was not always successful, was to try to avoid any large towns or cities. It meant the journey was slow but one was privileged to see much more of the country.

The photograph on the right shows the dogs on the top deck of the 12.40 P.&O. ferry on the trip to Calais. They look suitably unimpressed by the English Channel. Although they had been on ferries to and from the Isle of Wight on several occasions, they had tended to remain in the car below deck. This was the first time that they travelled on deck and could see the

water. It is always a struggle carrying a holdall and trying to manoeuvre ones way up or down several flights of narrow crowded stairs on a boat with two dogs on leads.

After disembarking at Calais I tentatively drove south aiming in the general direction of Samer. Unfortunately I encountered a cloudburst and became rather disorientated.

As a result I found myself unable to turn the car around, and at the start of a toll road that I had not really wanted to take. I came to a halt besides the ticket machine, which was on the passenger side of the car, with the rain hammering upon the roof of the car, with rivers of water gushing across the road and with a queue forming behind me. It was impossible to reach the ticket machine from inside the car, and so I had no option but to get soaked to the skin. It was not an auspicious start to our holiday.

Fortunately I arrived at my already booked destination of Madame Fourdinier's Gite de France within the hour and was able to completely change my clothes. Madame Fourdinier and her husband Michel have a small farm called La Ferme de Beauvois, which is about 30 miles south of Calais in the small village of Lacre. On the farm Michel rears cattle and has a small flock of goats. The photograph on the right shows Gemma and Benji eyeing up the Three Billy Goats Gruff.

The accommodation at the farm is very comfortable and is a great place to stay if you enjoy walking, as the nearest shop or bar is about five kilometres away in Samer. We had booked two nights in the smallest gite which had two bedrooms, a living room with a small television, a kitchenette, a shower and a toilet. I had stayed there at least twice before and although 'les animaux non acceptés' I had assured Danielle that my dogs were extremely well behaved Border Collies and would not be allowed in the bedrooms, despite Gemma's love of comfort. We must have made a very good impression as we were welcomed back two years later with no questions asked.

It is a little ironic really but I felt that the liveliest place in Lacre seemed to be the graveyard which always had amazing floral displays on nearly every grave, whilst in a corner of the cemetery were the well-tended graves of three British Tommies from the First World War. The village, however, is within easy reach of Boulogne, Le Touquet, Montreuil and the Welsh fish and chip shop in Etaples.

The next stage in the journey was to travel about 280 miles south to Le Moulin du Prieuré, in Dissay-Sous-Courcillon, where I had stayed before. It lies in the heart of the marvellous Loire chateau country and is the home of Marie-Claire, who spoke excellent English and had a very large B&B, which covered two sites and which offered a wide range of accommodation. She also provided delicious French meals in the evening if required.

The main section of the Bed and Breakfast was an old mill which was originally owned by the nearby Priory. It had been built by Augustin monks in the 12th century and had become a luxurious B&B. Quite a substantial tributary of the Loir runs through the extensive gardens and was used to power the waterwheel to which the dogs were attached in the photograph on the previous page. The room to the left of the wheel was the dining area which housed the ancient wooden wheel that used to grind the corn.

I had decided to stay there two days so that I could visit the chateau of Le Lude which lies about 15 miles to the west of Dissay along the Loir. It was a place that I had visited with one of my friends from college in 1965. Four of our fellow students were studying for a year in Tours and we decided to visit them. Unfortunately we failed to find them and ended up in Le Lude where we were too poor to visit the chateau, which was performing an amazing Son et Lumiere. Although the chateau was closed to visitors when I visited, the gardens were certainly worth the visit and the chateau looked magnificent.

Early that Saturday morning we left Dissay knowing that it would take the best part of two days to travel the 450 miles to Grenoble. I drove for about 300 miles that day in a southeasterly direction towards the Massif Central before finding a Premiere Classe Hotel on an industrial estate near Clermont-Ferrand.

TIP NUMBER 23: When driving through France, Industrial Estates are great places to find cheap hotel rooms in B&B Hotels, Ibis, or Premier Classe Hotels and dogs are usually welcome for a small fee (circa 4 euros per night).

After a nightmare drive through the busy traffic of Grenoble my Sat Nav, with the voice of John Cleese, guided me to my destination at Jolyon's flat which was built in 1968 to house competitors at the Winter Olympic. After a brief cup of tea we were back on the road again with Corinne as my guide to drive the 30 miles to St. Andeol. The final five kilometres from St. Guillaume to St. Andeol was quite a breath-taking climb as the road zig-zagged repeatedly as it climbed several hundred feet. On one side of the car was a sheer rock face whilst on the other side lay death and destruction.

The chalet, whose photograph is on the previous page, was at a height of about three thousand feet and sat beside a narrow road which ascended another half mile to the village of St. Andeol, where the only buildings of note were the church, the mayor's house and a Centre de Vacances for school children.

The photograph on the left-hand side, on the previous page, shows the rear view of the chalet which had been built into a steep slope. From the front it appeared to be a three storey building with a garage and store room on the ground floor, but at the rear only two floors were visible. The living room and its balcony, the kitchen, the bathroom and my bedroom were on the first floor, whilst two tiny bedrooms were in the attic. The two acre garden, which sloped steeply up from the road, was long and narrow and stretched for about a hundred yards.

As Jolyon and Corinne both had to return to Grenoble to work after le weekend, I was left to my own devices for most of the week. As the only shop and bar was in St. Guillaume at the foot of the valley I soon got to grips with tackling the perilous descent. If one wanted an English newspaper, a supermarket, a chemist, a doctor or a Post Office one had to travel about twelve kilometres to Monestier de Clermont which had a population of about 1,400. I seemed to travel there almost every other day.

It was a spartan life in the chalet and I soon found out that I was working almost as hard there as at home. The only heating in the chalet was the log burning fire in the living room which had to be cleaned out daily, and then relit again using the large pile of logs which lay under the eaves of the house. Meals had to be made three times a day, and washed up in a tiny sink. Any clothes that needed washing had to be washed

by hand and hung out to dry on the balcony. Whenever the dogs went out they seemed to get muddy, which meant there were numerous towels to wash.

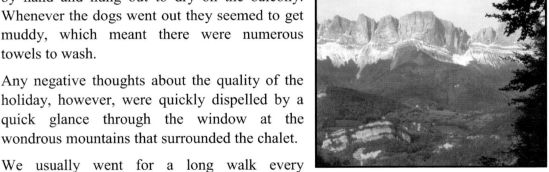

Any negative thoughts about the quality of the holiday, however, were quickly dispelled by a quick glance through the window at the wondrous mountains that surrounded the chalet.

We usually went for a long walk every afternoon as there were so many trails to investigate in the hills and the valleys where the dogs could be released, although I was very wary over the safety of my dogs as we were a long way from any veterinarian help. The steep slopes and precipitous sided valleys scared me the most, although I was also very worried by the small groups of heavily armed hunters and their baying hounds which we regularly came across. What was to stop them accidentally shooting me or my dogs, or having their enormous hounds rip my dogs apart? In a way it was less stressful walking along the narrow roads where if one saw a car it was a surprise.

On a couple of occasions we drove across the valley through Chateau Bernard to The Two Sisters, the mountains that I could see from my bedroom window. There the Col de l'Arzelier passed through the mountains at a height of 1154 metres. It was possible to park at the ski resort near the Col as there was no snow at that level in early October and the pistes were still a verdant green. From there we walked up to the top of the ski lift which was a further 1,200 metres up the mountain, to a small café from where, in the distance, it was possible to see Mont Blanc. It was an exhausting climb to the café and took the best part of ninety minutes to accomplish. But a beer for me and

water for the dogs made the effort worthwhile. The dogs wre lying beside the café at the top of the ski lift in the photograph.

In the evenings after I had cooked a meal, fed the dogs, washed up and built up the fire again, it was time to relax. For me relaxation involved trying to find a programme that I could understand on the tiny television which had five channels and poor reception. When that failed I resorted to reading one of the many books that I had brought with me. Trying to get the internet on my laptop was impossible.

For the dogs relaxation meant lying upon the rather spartan wickerwork settee which was on the far side of the room from the television. To reach it one had to pass the sometimes roaring log fire. Whilst Benji was quite happy to walk past the fire, Gemma always skirted around the outside of the room to reach her destination.

I must admit that the prospect of going to bed in the chalet was not one I looked forward to as the temperature plummeted towards freezing. Whilst the living room was relatively warm because of the log fire, and the two small bedrooms upstairs benefitted from rising heat, my bedroom had no heating. I slept in a sleeping bag with a hot water bottle on a ten inch high bed, over which was thrown an eiderdown. Gemma did her best to help keep me warm by sleeping beside me whilst Benji seemed happy enough lying by the wall on a dog blanket. Getting up in the middle of the night to go to an even colder toilet was not an experience to be relished. Neither was the thought that the mice, who had come into the house because of the cold, who one could occasionally hear tap-dancing on the stove in the kitchen, might decide to inspect the bedroom.

At the weekend Jolyon and Corinne arrived for a couple of days. Jolyon was an extremely fit tri-athlete who would regularly run or cycle around the Vercors in the summer, whilst in the winter he would ski. He knew the names of all the mountains, their heights and the passes through them and insisted on taking us on what I often considered were extremely dangerous walks for the dogs. Most of the time I kept Benji on the lead as I knew that Gemma would not stray too far away. It was also easier only having to keep an eye on one dog. The photograph on the right shows Jolyon and Corinne with the dogs in front of Mont-Aiguille  (2,086m) on the road leading out of Gresse-en-Vercors, which has a monument to all their members of the French Resistance who were executed in the village during the war.

On Sunday morning we went into Monestier de Clermont to visit the open air market, where Corinne purchased all the food that they needed for the following week in Grenoble. Whilst she watched television and then prepared a meal in the afternoon, Jolyon and I played boules and then indulged in football with the dogs. In the evening Corinne presented us with a fine pork based French meal, whilst Jolyon regaled us with his extensive knowledge of French wine and cheese.

The following week was a carbon copy of the first week and passed without any notable incident. It was a very quiet and relaxing fortnight. The nearest chalet was over two hundred yards away and some days passed without me speaking to a single sole apart from Benji and Gemma, who seemed to love the place.

 Jolyon and Corinne returned the following Friday evening so that I could spend my final few hours at the chalet with them. On the Saturday we went a walk along the River Gresse and had another game of boules in the afternoon. When I began to pack some of my bags into the car, the dogs seemed to sense that we were going to leave, and poor Benji looked quite sad as he sat under a tree in the garden. He was always a sensitive soul.

The first evening on the return trip was spent in a Premiere Classe Hotel at Monteau which is just to the north of Auxerre. On the following day I had intended to try to take a circuitous route well to the North of Paris but failed disastrously, and found myself heading into the heart of Paris in the evening rush hour. I only realised how close I was to the centre of Paris when I looked over my shoulder and saw the Eiffel Tower looming large about 200 yards away. It was a nightmare which I somehow survived, although I was honked at by several angry French motorists.

After spending that night in a B&B near Amiens we had made the return trip to Madame Fourdinier's slightly quicker than anticipated and, as a result, managed to spend an extra day there which gave us the chance to visit Le Touquet, where unfortunately I had no money left to spend in the Casino. The photograph on the right shows Benji and Gemma in front of the Casino Du Palais.

On the final day in France we had to make a sixty mile round journey to visit Dr. Herrewyn, a Veterinaire in the Boulevard Lafayette in Calais. It was the nearest practice that I could find in the telephone directory, and at least the receptionist spoke English. The motorway approaching Calais is not one that I love as the traffic is usually frenetic with lorry drivers and holiday makers rushing at breakneck speed to the port or the tunnel.

It was a legal requirement to visit the vet before returning to England in order that the dogs could be scanned and wormed by a vet, who would hopefully sign their passports declaring that *"The animal is in good health and able to withstand carriage to its destination."*

The following day I had to repeat the journey to Calais to catch the 11.40 ferry. The most worrying incident that day was when I was asked by a customs' official to scan the chips in my dogs' necks with a small handheld scanner. I think the battery in the device must have been nearing the end of its life as it took me three or four attempts to get a reading for Gemma. With Benji I could not get a reading. The custom official was becoming irritated, whilst I was beginning to panic and fully expected that we might have to spend another day or two in Calais. There was a genuine flood of relief when that 15 digit number eventually appeared on the screen.

Return to Les Vercors 2010

I had obviously enjoyed my trip to France with Benji and Gemma in 2008 as two years later I decided not only to repeat the experience, but chose to stay for five weeks. As the dogs were both twelve years old by that stage and both had health problems, I felt that it might be the last holiday that we might spend together.

Following an early start from Cheam to beat the rush hour we eventually caught the 12 o'clock ferry, the 'Pride of Calais' on September 28th and stayed that evening in the Gite of Madame Fourdinier before travelling 250 miles south the following day to lodge at Le Moulin du Prieuré in Dissay-sous-Courcillon with Marie Claire. I am nothing but predictable.

The first three days of our 2010 visit to France, therefore, followed a rather predictable pattern and must have been remarkably boring for the dogs as they spent at least twenty hours cooped up on the back seat of the car as we covered 700 miles at a snail's pace, as I was forever pulling into laybys either to check maps or to allow impatient French men and women to overtake.

On the third day after driving slowly eastwards for eight hours we found ourselves ensconced in quite a pleasant B&B Hotel on an industrial estate at Bourg les Valence. Up until that point nothing of note had occurred and we were on course to arrive a day early. The fourth day of our journey, however, was one of the most nerve-racking days that I have ever experienced and still sends a shiver down my spine whenever I think of what might have happened.

As I had plenty of time to complete the journey I made the fatal decision that it would be interesting to make a detour towards Gap and approach Grenoble from a southerly direction. We left Valence shortly after breakfast when I considered that the local rush hour had stopped, and I put my trust in John Cleese, the voice of my Tom Tom Sat Nav, to guide me safely towards Gap. John, however, had other ideas. As we travelled along the D91 the Sat Nav decided that the shortest distance between two points was a not very straight line.

As a result I found myself climbing a long narrow zig zag road, with the names of cyclists painted in whitewash on the tarmac, with no way of escape. The road was about four or five metres wide with no barrier on the right hand side to prevent one from plunging hundreds of feet to ones death. As I suffer from vertigo, I must admit I was petrified and decided that if I came across a car coming down the mountain road I would deliberately cross over to the wrong side of the road to hug the mountainside. There was no way I would try to pass another vehicle on the right hand side.

The road which climbed over 600 metres was eight and a half kilometres long, and the nightmare seemed to last for ever as we crawled slowly and carefully to the summit of the Col de Pennes (1040 metres) without fortunately seeing another car. At the summit was a small car park which contained one vehicle, a large van which had transported a crew of workmen to the site. I was extremely thankful that I had not encountered that van on the road as there was no way that we could have passed each other.

The workmen seemed rather surprised to see an Englishman and two dogs suddenly appear in the tiny car park. I stopped there for several minutes to regain my equilibrium, to stretch my legs and to walk the dogs. The photograph on the right shows Benji in the car park at the Col de Pennes waiting to climb back into the car, totally oblivious to the danger which we had faced.

The twelve kilometre descent down the east side of the col was much easier as the right hand side of the road seemed to hug the side of the mountain. There were, however, a couple of nervous moments when we encountered two vehicles, a car and a motorbike. As a result of my encounter with the Col de Pennes, I decided to forget about Gap and headed straight towards Grenoble where I booked into a rather upmarket Premiere Classe Hotel in Grenoble Sud.

There was a slight surprise for us the following day when we arrived at St. Andeol as there had been a dusting of snow the previous evening. The snow did not last long as the daily temperature rose to about 20*C, but at least the dogs seemed to enjoy it while it lasted. The photograph on the right shows Corinne, Benji, Gemma and myself crossing the field above the chalet.

We quickly fell into the same old routine. For most of the week we lived in splendid isolation and at the weekend Jolyon and Corinne joined us. This time, however, I came prepared with a small portable DVD player and a collection of films that I had never had time to watch at home. I had come to relax after a difficult and time consuming cricket season. One important difference on this trip, however, was that I became friends with the people in the nearest chalet, Jacques and Monique Picot, who had retired and were permanent residents in St. Andeol. Their chalet was luxurious in

comparison to the basic one in which I was living, and was even equipped with satellite television.

The photograph on the left shows me posing with the dogs on the steps of the chalet. Gemma looks far from happy.

Apart from Jacques and Monique inviting the dogs and myself to their beautiful chalet a couple of times for a meal of Pommes Dauphine, it was comforting to know that there was someone I could turn to if ever there was a problem. As Jacques had been an engineer he was able to fix any problem that arose in the chalet, whilst on one occasion I really found myself in need of Monique's nursing expertise.

One evening I was preparing a meal in the chalet of grilled steak and vegetables. The steak which I had purchased from the butcher in Monestier de Clermont had rather a thick rind of fat that I decided to remove using a small sharp knife. I had to exert a lot of pressure on the knife to make any impression upon the slice of meat. I was using a sawing action on the meat with my index finger on top of the blade when I suddenly noticed blood around my finger. The light had been so poor in the chalet that I had failed to notice that I had the knife upside down and that I had been pressing hard down upon the sharp side of the blade.

For a few minutes I panicked. There did not seem to be much choice: it was a twenty five minute drive to the nearest medical facility in Monestier, whilst I might struggle with my poor French to get medical help over the telephone. In the end, putting pressure upon the wound I walked the two hundred yards to the nearby chalet where Monique cleaned the cut, put a couple of Steri Strips across it and then bandaged it up. In the end it was only a minor emergency but it made me realise that if either the dogs or myself had a more serious accident then we were quite a long way from medical assistance.

Apart from that emergency there were only two other incidents of note. On one occasion whilst walking near Chateau Bernard Gemma accidentally fell into a sunken horse trough. As it was autumn, the road and the water in the trough were covered with a thick multicoloured layer of leaves. Gemma unfortunately tried to walk across the leaves on top of the horse trough and ended up being completely immersed. Thankfully she was almost dry by the time that we reached the chalet.

The second incident of note was the fact that my elderly dogs had managed to climb, rather slowly, to the Refuge at the top of the ski lift at the Col de l'Arzelier. Half way up the steep slope we halted and rested for a while. The photograph on the left shows a rather tired Gemma panting as she rested upon the grassy slope.

I then gave them the choice and asked them which way they wanted to go. To my surprise they both started to climb up the path again. Whether they really understood me, I do not know.

As we approached the café two large dogs, one a husky, suddenly bounded up to us and, for a few seconds, I feared that we might be attacked as Benji took an instant dislike to them. Fortunately the owner of the Refuge appeared and called his dogs away and locked them in a small wooden shed. Although I felt sorry for the dogs being locked away in a windowless hut on a very hot day, I was relieved that Benji and Gemma had survived the encounter unscathed.

The photograph on the right shows two extremely tired dogs resting on the rather rickety wooden floor of the Refuge with Mont Blanc in the distance. The owner of the Refuge had kindly provided them with a bowl of water whilst I sampled a glass of 5.8% proof Mandrin, the only alcoholic drink available.

The dogs loved living in the chalet. For much of the time I left the back door open which allowed them easy access to the garden whenever they needed to relieve themselves, which in Benji's case was quite often as he was forever marking his territory.

The garden was also the perfect place to play with a ball or to just chill out, whenever one needed to escape from the noise of Jolyon's extensive vintage CD collection.

If the back door was closed Benji loved to patrol the wooden balcony, where he sometimes spotted an occasional pedestrian and his dog walking past. Gemma was less enthusiastic about walking on the balcony but was quite happy to stand in front of the fireplace and watch him, provided that the fire was not lit.

On the 26th of October, after hearing that snow was forecast I decided to return to the Nord-Pas de Calais by a circuitous route, travelling anti-clockwise around the vast conurbation that is Paris. It took me about four days to make the trip staying in B&Bs near Dijon, Chalons and Reims. Whilst in champagne country I took a detour to see the House of Drappier in Urville where I had bought several cases of vintage champagne to celebrate the millenium. Most of the bottles had been given to friends and relatives as Christmas presents, whilst the rest became undrinkable in my garage.

When we arrived back at the farm of Madame Fourdinier at Lacre, it was disappointing to find out the gites were fully booked, mainly by English tourists. She did, however, put me in touch with Madame Therese Dupont who lived in a beautiful gated property about a mile north of Samer. Although we only had a bedroom and there were no cooking facilities we stayed there almost a week. As a bonus Madame Dupont provided a sumptuous breakfast and we could communicate using Franglais.

With Madame Fourdinier we had had to communicate using my rather poor oral French and a dictionary of useful phrases.

At the rear of the property there was a long enclosed driveway/lane which led steeply uphill to a minor rural road. As the lane was completely enclosed it was an ideal place to let the dogs roam freely, particularly when I wanted them to go to the toilet late at night.

As there was no kitchen where I could cook a meal, in the evenings I tended to either snack on a baguette and cheese or wander up to Samer, where there was a hot dog van by the side of the road. The food from it tended to be plentiful but unappetising.

On a couple of occasions I drove into the outskirts of Boulogne-sur-Mer and ate on one occasion at McDonalds, and on another occasion at my favourite restaurant, the Buffalo Grill, which combines cheapish steaks with Country and Western music and art. The walls are decorated with colourful prints of some of the great nineteenth century American western artists such as Frederic Remington and Charles M. Russell.

During the day I tended to drive either to Le Touquet or to Montreuil-sur-Mer as both of these towns have a very strong English influence and one has no trouble in buying a wide range of English newspapers, plus most of the shopkeepers speak English. After a month of trying to communicate with the people in the Vercors it came as somewhat of a relief to be understood and vice-versa.

Our first visit to Le Touquet began at one of the golf courses basically so that I could say that I had been there, and where I enquired about the cost of a round. As I only had one club and very little money there was no danger of me playing. Then I walked two rather bored dogs along the beautiful boulevards with their exclusive stores and restaurants, whilst I went window shopping.

The dogs probably enjoyed Montreuil more as we strolled around the picturesque medieval streets and the grass covered walls that surround the town, where there has been a fort or castle for over a thousand years. The town has a very strong English influence as the Citadel became the headquarters of Sir Douglas Haig and his troops in the First World War. Benji and Gemma are resting before the statue erected to honour General Haig, in the photograph on the right.

On the 4th of November we had to make the unnerving journey to the Boulevard Lafayette in Calais again, and on that occasion we saw a Dr. Nowosad who wormed them and thankfully found them both fit enough to travel, although he noted that they

both had a heart murmur. He felt that Benji's murmur was particularly bad, which surprised me, as Benji had always appeared to have been the most active, and whereas Gemma had to be helped into the car, Benji could still jump onto the back seat without any assistance.

On the following day, after I had successfully scanned their chips, we returned to Dover on the 'Pride of Calais'. The photograph on the right shows a rather haggard looking Gemma sitting on the rear seat of the car as we waited for the ferry in Calais. It was the last holiday that we all took together.

Benji and Gemma Health Issues

In retrospect I should never have bought Benji and Gemma from a pet shop as they were both beset by a series of health problems, some of which were probably genetic. But there again I am glad that I did as they were both wonderful dogs whom it was a privilege to know.

In the first couple of years there were several minor health problems such as upset tummies for both of them, conjunctivitis for Benji, and Kennel Cough for Gemma. Their health check report from the Wingrave Vets, however, in 2000 revealed that they were both in good condition. According to Nick Dodds, the vet, "They could not be any fitter." Gemma who weighed 20 kilograms was slightly heavier than Benji who weighed 19.6 kilograms.

The first serious health problem, which was probably genetic, appeared during their annual check up in April 2003 when the dogs were five years old, and I was informed that Gemma had a heart murmur. This led to a series of tests and X-rays which resulted in her being put on Enacard tablets for the remainder of her life. Eighteen months later Benji was similarly diagnosed as having a heart murmur and, after another series of expensive tests, also ended up having to take Enacard. For both dogs it meant having to hide their tablets in tiny bread sandwiches every day for about eight years. Although they were both insured I had to foot part of the bill for their heart problem. The Wingrave Clinic was quite sympathetic and, as I was a valuable customer, allowed me a 20% discount upon the Enacard.

TIP NUMBER 24: When taking out insurance it is advisable to take out a lifetime cover for any disease rather than for a limited sum.

At this point I think that it should be stressed how important it is to insure ones pet if one is to look after it responsibly. It is, however, vital to shop around for the best deal and to remember that the premiums always increase with age. When Benji and Gemma arrived they already had insurance from Four Paws at the reasonable cost of £224.40 for the pair of them. By the time that they were two years old I had switched their insurance to one offered by my bank and the cost began to sky-rocket annually.

After a cricket tour to Dorset ended in 2009 I came home to find a rather worrying letter from the insurance company with yet another astronomical rise in premium for the dogs. I was that annoyed that I sent them a small spreadsheet which showed how their rates had increased every year and wrote: *"I didn't expect that you would try to claw back the cost of their treatment by such draconian rises in the premiums. Over the past 4 years their premiums have risen by 262% for Benji and 212% for Gemma."*

	2006-2007	2007-2008	2008-2009	2009-2010
Gemma	£334.62	£399.27	£543.07	£707.98
Benji	£390.80	£456.53	£612.11	£1,024.46
Total	£725.42	£855.80	£1,155.18	£1,732.44

By August 2011 Gemma's annual premium had risen to £1,637.09, whilst by 2013 Benji's premium was £2,041.56. Overall, despite having to pay the first £125 of every condition, I felt that it had been worthwhile to have insured them both.

Despite these heart problems Benji and Gemma were both very fit and agile and continued racing around chasing a ball or frisbee, although I made sure that they did not overstrain themselves. I was constantly complimented by strangers who were always impressed by how fit they looked. It is ironic to think that neither of them died from heart disease.

One day in 2004, I became extremely worried when I witnessed Gemma having an epileptic fit, a year after she had been diagnosed with a heart murmur. Fortunately, I knew what was happening and how to treat her as Ben had had fits for about fourteen years. Thankfully Gemma's fit seemed to be a one-off event, but there again one is never with a dog 24/7.

Not all of Benji's and Gemma's visits to the vet's could be linked to their genetic history. Some of it was due to my own negligence in looking after my dogs. When Gemma was first diagnosed with a heart murmur, I was also warned that she had a build-up of tartar on her teeth. I obviously failed to heed this warning as, in September 2006, she had a couple of teeth removed. Four years later she was sedated again so that her teeth could be scaled and polished.

Although Benji did not have the same dental problems, probably because of his constant chewing of his fleece, he did have several serious health problems. On two occasions when he was eight years old he was operated on to remove skin tumours. The photograph on the right shows a six inch scar running along his throat which was caused when he had a spindle cell tumour removed. Thankfully he was very good at not scratching the scar as it was not in a great place for him to wear a plastic Elizabethan cone or collar.

Prior to these operations Benji had been quite relaxed whenever we visited the Wingrave surgery in Mulgrave Road, Sutton. Shortly afterwards, however, when we went for a check-up I noticed that his attitude had changed. The waiting room was full of patients and we had to wait over twenty minutes. Benji sat there shaking until eventually he suffered from a bout of diarrhoea. He had gone in for a check-up and ended being treated for a stomach disorder.

Following this incident it was decided that it might be advisable to visit the Wingrave's surgery at Court Rec. in Epsom, which was much brighter, quieter and rarely had more than a couple of patients waiting to be seen. The transformation in his behaviour was amazing. Whenever we visited there, although he might be seeing the same vet, he was calm and relaxed again. Over fifteen years later I am still taking my dogs to the Epsom branch.

Towards the end of 2010 it was obvious that Gemma had a problem with her breathing, which was not helped by the constant and excessive nasal discharge from which she appeared to suffer. All attempts to cure her by the vets at the Wingrave Hospital failed and so they referred her to the North Downs Specialist Referrals Unit at Bletchingley, where she stayed for three nights in January 2011. Whilst there she underwent various blood tests, rhinoscopy and a CT-Scan at a cost of over £2,600.

Gemma presented a sorry sight when she returned home, having had her forehead shaven. Although there was some improvement in her condition she seemed to lack her former sparkle, which was not helped by her being put on pain killers for a spinal condition. Gradually by the following Christmas it was obvious that Gemma's kidneys were failing and she was struggling to walk.

It was with a feeling of trepidation that I took her to see Birgitte Sims at the Wingrave Surgery in Epsom on December 30th, 2011. Birgitte explained that it would be a kindness to curtail her suffering by putting her to sleep. Therefore, at 3.35p.m. that day, Gemma breathed her last in my arms with her brother by her side. Birgitte thought that it was important that Benji witnessed what happened to Gemma, as it might help him come to terms with her death. The photograph on the right was taken earlier that day as Benji and Gemma, like an old married couple, watched life passing by in the Close, together for the last time.

When we arrived home I gently placed Gemma's body in the garage and went upstairs and slumped into my usual chair in the living room, whilst Benji went and sat on the settee in the spot where Gemma usually lay. He sat there, bolt upright for a minute in silent tribute to his dead sister just looking at me as though to say, "She's gone!" He then jumped off the settee and never sat there again.

The following day, New Year's Eve, we drove down to Oakwood Hill to my cousin Juliet's farm where Gemma was buried in a field where she had loved to run freely chasing a ball or a frisbee and, while we dug the grave, Benji lay there quietly watching as his sister was laid to rest. In the grainy photograph on the right one can just about see a single pink rose on her grave.

It was, I felt, the end of an era. I had been privileged to look after a pair of sibling Border Collies, despite being warned that it was a bad idea. They brought so much joy into the lives of everyone they met.

Benji and Poppi - A Collie with Attitude

In the days after Gemma's death Benji was very quiet and withdrawn and I became very concerned about him. The only solution was to find him another companion. I, therefore, began to trawl my way through various Border Collie rescue centres on the internet within a couple of weeks, and eventually stumbled across Poppi, a tri-coloured bitch, who had arrived at the Border Collie Trust GB near Rugeley in Staffordshire on January 23rd, 2012, on account of her aggressive behaviour.

I do not know why I was attracted to her as the photograph on the right was rather grainy and she was colour coded 'Blue': which meant that she was *'A dog who has a history of, or has displayed a higher degree of problem behaviour. The reasons for this can be varied. Generally fairly experienced homes only with no young children on a regular basis but again this is dependant on all the circumstances. These dogs will certainly require time, patience and compassion but can be a very rewarding experience."* The final sentence was so very true. I can now look back upon her life and realise how rewarding it was to have known Poppi, and how sorry I now feel for the family who had to relinquish her.

On Wednesday January 28^{th,} 2012, it took Benji and myself over four hours to drive to the Border Collie Trust G.B. at Colton. The Rescue Centre was very impressive which is more than I could have said for Poppi, who stood there very quietly with her ears flattened. The photograph on the left shows her being held by one of the staff at the centre whilst I was being introduced to her.

Even when I took her a short walk she seemed very disinterested in me or her surroundings. She was obviously traumatised at having been separated from the family who had loved and cared for her since they had bought her from a breeder when she was 13 weeks old.

Poppi's history

As I read the copious notes upon Poppi, which had been furnished by the previous owner, I began to feel really sorry for the dog, who had been abandoned by her family. Poppi had spent three and a half years in what seemed to be a busy loving home with three adults, one of whom was a grandmother who worked from home, and two girls aged eleven and fifteen. She appeared to have been a rather friendly dog with the members of her family and allowed them to take food and bones away from her and loved to play with a ball. The notes also revealed that she would occasionally jump into the rabbit hutch but never tried to harm the rabbit.

Apparently Poppi had been very protective towards members of the family, especially in the presence of strange men, and she would growl and show her teeth at any workmen who entered the house. There had been, however, a couple of more serious incidents involving members of the family. On one occasion Poppi was lying close to the front door when an aunt wanted to leave the house. She told Poppi to move and pointed. Poppi rose to her feet and snapped at the hand before going to her basket.

The straw that broke the camel's back, however, occurred shortly before she was sent to the Rescue. In the notes written by the mother it said, *"Poppi was lying near the bedroom door and my daughter (15) came out of her room, caught the dog with the door. She jumped up at her and bit her thigh. It hurt but did not break the skin."* The fifteen year old daughter, who sounded rather spoiled, kicked up a fuss and insisted that the parents got rid of Poppi.

The notes also revealed that the family must have spent a considerable amount of time training her as she knew numerous commands, did not pull on the lead, was house trained, travelled quietly in the car, came back when called and was usually good with other dogs. She was, however, apparently scared of fireworks and loud noises.

The notes provided by the Centre said that Poppi was a *"very nervous and cautious dog, needs time and patience to recover from past stress. Doesn't trust easily, so time and patience is needed to form a bond or relationship with her. Seems a very sensitive dog."*

After paying the Centre the £150 rehoming fee, a member of the staff led Poppi out to my car where she seemed quite content to jump into the empty luggage bay behind the rear seat where Benji was lying. I was asked to bring her back if there was a problem with her. I said that I felt that was unlikely as it was a 300 mile round trip.

The most memorable incident on the trip back to Cheam occurred after about twenty minutes when I spotted, in the rear view mirror, that Benji had stood up and looked over the back of the seat and then immediately sat down. One could almost imagine a speech bubble coming out of his head which said, "I'm right! He's put a bloody dog in the boot!"

When we arrived home I took both dogs into the garden so that they could wee and then took them into the house. At her previous home in Syston Poppi had been barred from going upstairs by a small gate. To be free to go up two flights of stairs was certainly a novelty for her and I left her free to investigate her new home. That was a rookie mistake as I found out when I ventured onto the top landing and found a small pile of poo. So that is what she thought of her new home!

Poppi - a Complex Canine

Although Poppi often appeared to be a very confident and aggressive dog, behind that façade lay a more timid animal, as I found out the first time that I took her into the park and she tried to flee when a car back-fired. Any loud noise scared her. If a firework exploded whilst she was in the garden, she would throw herself through the dog flap, run upstairs and seek refuge on her bed in the living room, where she would lie frozen still upon her stomach and paws, with her ears flattened.

Poppi was also very sensitive towards the weather. I noticed that she would become very quiet if the atmospheric pressure was low or if it was hot and sultry. Perhaps she realised that these conditions were often the sign that a storm might be imminent, or perhaps she could hear thunder in the distance. She quickly showed that she understood the word 'bangs', which I used to refer to thunder and fireworks.

Her acute hearing could have been the reason that she spent a considerable amount of time gazing into the sky at passing aeroplanes. She maintained this habit throughout her life which led me to wonder if her previous home in Syston had been on a flight path to Birmingham airport.

Poppi - the Companion

The main reason for rescuing Poppi had been to provide Benji with a companion as he had been devastated by the loss of his sister. For the first fortnight he tried unsuccessfully to avoid contact with Poppi, who quickly tried to dominate him by occasionally nipping him and trying to mount him. Although Benji turned on her twice and threw her, screaming, to the floor with his teeth at her throat, it had absolutely no affect upon her as she persisted in her attempts to dominate him for at least the first two months. Having her in the house, however, helped Benji recover from the loss of Gemma. Poppi was impossible to ignore!

The photograph on the left was one of the first that was taken of the dogs together after Poppi's arrival. Their relationship looks decidedly frosty.

It soon became evident, however, that the dogs had actually built up a working relationship. When I played ball with Poppi in the garden Benji would bark encouragement, whilst she stopped trying to mount him and only nipped him occasionally. She would often wander up to him with her tail wagging and give his head a sniff, and seemed to realise that the pills that he received were for him alone and made no attempt to take them. Poppi did not seem at all worried by the fact that Benji was always fed first but would sit there patiently waiting her turn. If she finished her food before him she did not try to get his food, but if he failed to catch a treat, however, then it was hers.

The photograph on the right shows a much more confident Poppi after she had been with us for seven months. Her ears were pricked up, she looked alert and was definitely rather scruffy, as she detested being brushed or combed. She also wore the RAC harness nearly all of her life as she was a frequent traveller in the car, plus the strap on the top of the harness was ideal to grab hold of, if one wanted to control her quickly.

The photograph of Benji on the left was taken on the same warm September day in 2012. Although he was beginning to look rather old he still retained his brilliant symmetrical facial markings and there was a surprising absence of grey.

Although Benji and Poppi slept in different rooms they often sought each other out for company during the daytime and were both usually found lying together behind the front door whenever I returned home. As Benji was rather deaf and could not hear me shouting I often had to ask Poppi to fetch him. She would run downstairs barking and if that failed she would give him a nip.

Poppi and Postmen

Poppi did not like postmen. If she looked through the window and saw a postman approaching the house she would bark, run downstairs and snatch and shake any letters put through the post-box. On one occasion I tried to make her befriend the postman. She actually allowed him to stroke her but when he moved to post a letter next door she ran after him, jumped up and nipped him.

Any postman that we passed in the street would elicit the same reaction. Poppi would bark and lunge towards him. It was not just postmen who annoyed her, but any workman in a high viz jacket such as a dustman or a delivery driver. Postwomen were usually safe. If, however, we walked past a disreputable looking person I had to keep a tight hold on the lead in case she attacked him. I must admit that on several occasions when she lunged at a passing stranger I had every sympathy with her as I usually did not like his look either. I did, however, feel perfectly safe as I fought to drag my snarling protector away. She was a very ferocious looking dog! This behaviour became less noticeable as she aged and became more confident in her surroundings.

Poppi an aggressive dog

Poppi also bit me at least twice in our first month together. On one occasion I tried to pull her off a bed as she refused to get down, and on the other occasion I tried to drag her out of the car. I must admit that it happened so quickly and was quite scary, but did not hurt. In a split second her teeth would gently latch onto my hand. It was her way of warning me that she was not happy, and that she could really do some damage if she felt so inclined. I soon learnt to spot the warning signs - the twitching of the upper lip and the baring of the teeth. Over the years she probably 'bit' me hundreds of times, particularly when I tried to either brush her or, in her later years, dry her paws. Whenever I dried her paws I was in the habit of whispering to her 'no bite, no bite'.

Poppi had only been in Cheam about a week when she tried to attack a neighbour, who had unfortunately grabbed hold of her. Although she did not bite him, it did sour our relationship for a while as he threatened to kick her 'effing head in'. One visitor whom I did not want Poppi to bite, however, was our milkman, Michael Gray, He did, however, succeed in winning her over by coming armed with Bonios. She still jumped up at him and looked scary, but it was a welcoming jump.

Poppi was a great guard dog. In warm weather I was perfectly happy to leave the front door of the house open as she enjoyed sleeping at the foot of the stairs. When anyone tried to open the porch door she would go ballistic and appeared to be ultra-aggressive. Unwanted callers were encouraged to leave by my holding Poppi by the harness as though I was struggling to restrain a vicious hound.

Poppi and Visitors

Whenever a visitor was invited into the house Poppi's demeanour changed from one of aggression to that of welcome. Her first reaction was to find a ball and to drop it at the guest's feet in the hope that they would either kick or throw it. She even greeted

any workmen in the same fashion, which was rather strange when one considered the notes which had been provided by her previous family in Syston, which stated that she was aggressive towards workmen. As her family in Syston had been mainly female, however, it could have been that she was trying to protect them, whereas she was not interested in protecting me.

One of my regular visitors who lived in Finchley, was my nephew Neil, an award winning composer of film music, his Korean wife Seon-Ju, and their young son Sam. Seon-Ju and Sam were literally terrified of Poppi and would not come into the house until Poppi had calmed down. Benji, in his turn, always left the room when they arrived. I think that he realised that when he played around small children, they usually ended up crying and he ended up being told off. It was, therefore easier to avoid them,

Neil would spend most of the visit just kicking or throwing a ball into the dining room to keep Poppi occupied and away from his family, whilst if ever we went into the park Neil was always the person that Poppi chose to throw a stick for her.

Neil's brother, Matthew, suffered a rather traumatic experience at the hands, or teeth, of Poppi when he stayed with me in 2013. Matthew, a six feet tall student in his mid-twenties who looked like he could take care of himself, had come to London to study and take a Master's degree. As he seemed to get on very well with Poppi, I had no qualms in leaving them together one Saturday afternoon whilst I went off to play cricket.

When I returned to the house I was greeted, by a very friendly dog at the foot of the stairs, as though she were extremely pleased to see me and to tell me that nothing out of the ordinary had happened that day. Matthew came out of the downstair's bedroom where he had been trapped by Poppi for most of the afternoon and informed me of what had really happened.

Earlier that afternoon Matthew had accidentally left the front door open and Poppi had gone walkabout. When he found that she was missing he walked down to the park and discovered her just inside the entrance. He made the fatal error of grabbing her, whereupon she bit him.

Somehow he managed to return her to the house but, by this time, the damage was done. Poppi realised that he was scared of her and took great delight in dominating him. She stood at the bottom of the stairs snarling and growling whenever he tried to go upstairs. The only way that he could pass her was by climbing over the banister. When I returned she was all sweetness and light, and from her demeanour it appeared that the two of them had spent a very pleasant afternoon together. She did not seem to realise that Matthew 'grassed' upon her through the medium of the spoken word.

Poppi at the Vets

On our first visit to the Wingrave vets in Epsom we were met by a pleasant New Zealand vet called Aaron. I had already put a canvas muzzle on Poppi and she seemed very quiet and calm in the surgery until Aaron put on his stethoscope and tried to listen to her heart. She went bananas and tried to attack him. As a result he had to put a Baskerville muzzle over the top of the canvas one and I had to try to hold her steady. As soon as the stethoscope disappeared, however, she became a quiet well behaved dog, who expected a biscuit. I do not think that any vet ever managed to listen to her heart for more than about five seconds, and she always had to wear two muzzles before she was examined.

The other vet at the practice, Birgitte, was even more damning about Poppi and said that there was a certain look in her eyes that she did not trust, and that I should always muzzle her whenever I took her out. The photograph on the right shows a muzzled Poppi at Carisbrook Castle later that summer. The muzzle only remained in place for a few months. After that I preferred to keep her on a short lead and to warn anyone who might want to stroke her that she might be aggressive, although she never was.

We did, however, decide that it might be a good idea to have Poppi visit the surgery as often as possible just to get a treat, in order that she associated the place with a pleasant experience. For her first year with me I tended to make the eight mile round trip to Epsom at least three times a week just to weigh her and to get a treat. In the end she really loved visiting the surgery and was as good as gold unless she was being poked or prodded or saw the stethoscope, in which case two muzzles had to be applied.

One very important outcome of these first encounters with the Wingrave vets was that her medical record had her listed as being a dangerous dog. It was a label which was to result in her being wrongly denied treatment by a specialist veterinarian practice several years later. It was a case of giving a dog a bad name.

TIP NUMBER 25: If your dog is scared of visiting the vets, try taking him/her there more often just to get a treat, and hopefully the dog will associate the place with a pleasant experience.

Poppi in the Park

Poppi loved chasing a ball in the park whilst Benji ran slowly after her. She seemed to have given him a new lease of life. Passers-by found it hard to believe that he was over fourteen years old and had been on heart tablets for over half of his life.

If no ball was available in the park Poppi would nearly always find a stick. Sometimes it was a small stick about two or three feet in length which she would grip in the middle and run around with her head thrown backwards. Occasionally she would find what could only be described as being a large branch which she would grip tightly in her mouth and, with her head tilted over her shoulder, she would run around supporting the weight of the branch on her back. She was incredibly strong and could drag branches that I struggled to lift.

I tried, without success, to stop her playing with sticks as I felt that they could injure her. As I refused to throw sticks for her she would often drop them in front of complete strangers in the hope that they would play with her.

The two stick related photographs in this section have been taken from a video of Poppi's first and only visit to Marsden Park in Nelson in the summer of 2013.

I already knew that Poppi loved playing with water as she would attack the spray which came out of the hosepipe whenever I tried to water the garden. It was on that visit to Nelson that I also discovered that Poppi was a very good swimmer.

In Marsden Park there is a beautiful, large ornamental pond where I used to fish for minnows, sticklebacks or frogspawn as a child. Before I knew what was happening Poppi had dived into the water about two hundred yards away from me and started to swim towards some ducks. When I shouted at her she turned around in the water and swam to the stone-lined edge of the lake which was a good foot above the water level. The water must have been too deep for her to stand on

the bottom of the pond and, although she managed to get her front feet onto the bank, she could not pull herself out with her paws. She then started to swim around the edge of the pond.

Fortunately I was there to save her, and whilst holding my video camera in my left hand, I grabbed her harness and pulled her out with my right hand. As thanks she soaked me as she repeatedly shook herself, and for the following twenty minutes she spent the time rolling repeatedly down a grassy bank in a vain attempt to dry herself. The photograph on the left which was taken from the video shows one damp and bedraggled dog.

After this incident I always put a tight rein on her if ever there was a pond or river in the vicinity. She obviously loved the water, and whenever she travelled on a ferry she seemed to look at the expanse of water with great longing.

I also had to be careful whenever Poppi was off the lead, if other dogs were around, as one never knew how she would react, as it seemed to be in her nature to try and dominate any dog who had the temerity to invade her space. She would often show her teeth and snap at dogs who came close to her, but never became involved in a serious fight. It was, however, occasionally embarrassing if one was talking to a fellow dog walker, with both dogs on their respective leads, when Poppi suddenly decided to nip their precious pooch. Her unpredictability was one of the qualities that made Poppi the most challenging and interesting of my dogs.

Training Poppi to be less Aggressive

During our first few weeks together I discovered that Poppi had been really well trained by the family who had abandoned her. She would roll over on command and was more than happy to sit, stay, lie down and give one her paw. Although it was obvious that she was a little wary of walking beside the main road, she automatically stopped and sat at every junction, or before crossing the road. She made me feel guilty over my lack of success at training my dogs to do that.

Poppi's main problem was the way that she appeared to be aggressive towards workmen, strange men and other dogs in the street. To try to cure this tendency I made a point of taking Benji and Poppi, who was muzzled and on a short lead, into Cheam Village three or four times a week. We tended to end up in 'The Prince of Wales' where the dogs were usually welcomed by Ronnie, the barmaid, with a variety of treats. It was a welcoming environment which catered mainly for the working man.

Strange men were constantly walking past her in the pub, or stepping over her, or even making a fuss of her as they made their way to the toilet. Never once did she try to attack anyone. For the first few months Poppi was muzzled whenever we went into 'The Prince of Wales' but I eventually discarded the muzzle, although I was always on tenterhooks that she might blot her copybook and bite someone. Her attitude towards postmen and workmen in hi-viz jackets, however, never improved.

In order to try to improve her attitude towards other dogs I enrolled her on an agility course in May 2012 with Chantal Karita (later Chantal Catherine) in a field near 'The Cock' at Headley. We must have attended these classes for about six months with Benji tethered to a fence barking his support. As Poppi seemed to enjoy the agility and was one of the best in the class, despite her ancient owner who could not keep up with her, I bought her a few agility items so that we could practice in the park.

Poppi appeared to be tolerant of most of the dogs in the class apart from two black Labradors with whom she seemed to have a problem. Eventually a minor altercation erupted, for which Poppi was blamed, and I was asked to remove her from the course. How embarrassing to be kicked off the agility course!

Poppi and the Car

Poppi loved being in the car and would try to climb into it whenever an opportunity occurred. If ever a door was left ajar, or the boot was open and Poppi was in the vicinity, she would leap into the car and clamber on to the back seat, from where it was very difficult to remove her. I must admit that I was constantly worried that she might get into the car one day without my noticing and she might die from heat stroke..

It was usually a nightmare trying to remove Poppi from the car without getting bitten. I tried tempting her with treats, speaking to her firmly, squirting her with a water pistol, pleading with her, and as a final option I would attempt to attach a lead to her harness so that I could drag her out. If the weather was fine, however, I would sometimes open all the windows and the boot and leave her there. On one occasion I left her there for over six hours, visiting her every hour or so to see if she was ready to leave her comfortable seat.

There was never a problem leaving the windows of the car open whenever I parked the car with the dogs inside as Poppi was a great guard dog. Anyone who dared to stick their hand through the window, whether male or female, or even me, she would usually greet with the same aggressive response. On one occasion I pulled up close to Mike Byford, the Chairman of the Cricket Club, for a chat and wound down the front passenger window. Mike stroked Benji whilst we talked and then stretched his arm over the front seat to stroke Poppi. Before he knew what was happening Poppi's teeth were clamped firmly around his hand.

Whenever I had to take passengers to a cricket match I tended to load the passengers into the car first and then let Poppi climb in. When this happened her behaviour was usually exemplary and she would allow them to gently stroke her if they so desired. On one memorable occasion, however, I drove Jamie Anderson and Michael Prior down to play cricket at Mynthurst. Jamie sat in the front whilst Michael had the privilege of accompanying Poppi on the rear seat. After the game we went back to 'The Plough' in Leigh where we sat enjoying the hospitality of our opponents for a couple of hours.

At about nine o'clock we decided that it was time to leave. I gave Jamie and Michael the keys and told them to get into the car whilst I nipped to the toilet. When I came out I was surprised to see that they were both standing outside the car. When I asked them why they had not got into the car Jamie simply said, "Poppi bit Michael!"

Apparently as Poppi was lying across the whole of the back seat Michael had tried to push her across and she had reacted in her usual fashion.

Poppi was always so quiet in the car that it was sometimes easy to forget that she was there. That must have been the reason why I forgot that she was with me on one occasion, when I visited the Hyundai garage in Belmont with a minor electrical problem. One of the technicians took my car keys and drove the car into the inspection bay. When he returned he told me what the problem was and then said, "By the way I like your dog!" I was gobsmacked that I had firstly left the dog in the car, and that secondly she had allowed him to drive the car away. But there again she was always unpredictable.

Poppi's Occasional Manic Behaviour

Poppi quite often exhibited behaviour which appeared psychotic but it was probably only the result of her inherent traits. She would probably have been a great working sheep dog and occasionally she reverted to type. Sometimes it was as though a switch had been thrown and she would start pacing backwards and forwards or walking around in circles trying to round up Benji and myself.

Whenever I took the dogs into the park and their paws were muddy I would hose them down before trying to dry them in the conservatory. The photograph on the right shows them standing in the conservatory close to the door of the downstair's bedroom, waiting to be allowed into the house. The bamboo furniture was covered with white protective sheets which Poppi loved to pull off, whilst the mangle on the left was used as a  rack for towels, but could if needed be used as a tethering post.

Whenever I tried to dry Benji's paws first, Poppi would circle around us and the furniture in a frenzy and continually tried to nip in and snap at the old man. If I dried her paws first and let her into the house she would rotate at breakneck speed and bark aggressively from the other side of the strengthened glass door, against which she would occasionally throw herself.

On some occasions, particularly late at night, she would station herself by the open door that led into the conservatory and would pace backwards and forwards as though she was guarding us from some evil entity that lurked beyond.

Poppi's behaviour was usually exemplary when on a walk until she encountered an automated crossing. She would sit there quietly waiting to cross the road but as soon as the green man flashed and began to beep, she would drag me across the road and attack the box that emitted the noise. As soon as the noise stopped she would walk on, obviously satisfied that she had killed it. Although I tried to stop her, as it was quite embarrassing struggling to control an apparently mad dog, in front of an audience of waiting car drivers, she continued with this manic behaviour for the whole of her life. It was my behaviour rather than hers that altered, in that I tried whenever possible to avoid any automated crossing that I knew emitted a loud beeping sound.

Poppi - Impossible to Ignore

I often felt that Poppi's only role in life was to wind me up and create more work for me. Almost every day I would come across a bed in the house where the covers had been rucked up; in the living room the cushions were often thrown onto the floor from the settee: in the Conservatory she would drag the protective coverings off the furniture; in the bathroom she would remove the bar of soap from the side of the bath, chew it and leave it on the floor; in the downstairs toilet she would shake the mat at the base of the toilet and leave it in the corridor; she would also occasionally rip the piece of carpet off the wall behind which the stop cock was hidden; in the garden she would dig small holes in the gravel surrounding the path. If ever I saw her doing these things she would look at me as though to say, "So what are you going to do about it?" I spent most of my time trying to thwart her by placing flowerpots and bricks on the gravel and chairs on the beds.

Poppi also seemed to have a knack of opening the door between the conservatory and the house if the door was not firmly shut, which was sometimes rather exasperating if her paws were muddy. Occasionally she even managed to open one of the cupboard doors in the kitchen in which were stored dentasticks and treats. She was definitely a very inquisitive dog who loved pushing her way into any cupboard or drawer that I cared to open. Probably much of her seemingly bad behaviour was down to boredom.

She completely dominated Val, one of life's victims, who cleaned for me one day a week before Covid struck. Whenever she tried to vacuum the floor of the house where Poppi was lying, the dog would bare her teeth and snap at the nozzle of the vacuum. I seemed to be forever having to move Poppi for the terrified cleaner.

In the garden Poppi would circle around the mower or strimmer in a frenetic manner as I tried to cut the grass. That was before I had the small, poorly-kept lawn in the rear garden replaced by artificial grass in 2014, whilst the areas of the garden around the leylandii and to the right of the lawn were paved.

It was one of the best decisions that I ever made as the dogs no longer dirtied their paws in garden. Whenever the dogs went into the garden they tended to walk around the paved area and went to the toilet on the artificial grass. Any urine disappeared below the surface whilst the poo was very visible and could be easily picked up and placed into a special bin. After that the surface could be quickly hosed down, despite

Poppi trying to catch the spray, and one was left with a clean surface upon which to play. The photograph on the right shows Poppi waiting for me to start hitting golf balls into a net.

Poppi made trying to practice cricket or golf in the garden very difficult as she always wanted to join in and catch the ball. It was especially dangerous when she tried to stand in the centre of the golf net into which I was hitting golf balls. When I banished her from the net she would circle around the outside of the net and the mat from which I was hitting the balls. Even that was dangerous and I found myself

continually ordering her into the conservatory, where she would stay for a couple of minutes before venturing out to try to become involved again.

Whenever I tried to use a cricket catching frame in the garden Poppi would again try to stand between me and the frame. As this was also very dangerous if I was using a cricket ball, I usually had to resort to using a tennis ball where the object of the game was to try to miss the dog, and to hit the frame in such a way that the ball missed the dog on the way back. Quite often she caught the ball before it reached the frame. It certainly made the practice more entertaining and sharpened up ones reactions.

By the side of the conservatory, near the water butt, there was a small triangular area of artificial grass, which was the scene of a strange daily morning ritual for Poppi. After going to the toilet on the main lawn she would head towards that area of artificial grass, whereupon she would throw herself onto her back and roll over vigorously for about twenty seconds kicking the conservatory with her rear legs.

TIP NUMBER 26: There are many benefits to be gained from replacing your muddy dog-worn lawn with artificial grass. It may not be ecologically sound but it certainly makes life easier and makes the garden look very presentable.

Poppi's Behaviour at Cricket Matches and on the Golf Course

Poppi quickly learnt from Benji how to behave at cricket matches and would lie next to him, watching quietly from beyond the boundary. As Poppi loved being in the car I decided to take Benji and her for a week long cricketing holiday to the Isle of Wight in early September 2012, with members of the Surrey Seniors Cricket Association. The photograph on the right shows them both lying quietly watching a game at Ryde.

Poppi's behaviour at cricket matches was always impeccable and she gained many admirers. One of my abiding memories was of a teenage lad at Shanklin C.C. falling under her spell, and despite my warning him that she could be aggressive, he stroked her for over half an hour before telling his parents that he wanted a dog just like Poppi.

As Benji was reluctant to go to the golf club by this late stage in his life he could not teach Poppi the correct canine golfing etiquette. This meant that Poppi's behaviour on the golf course left much to be desired. Although she was securely tethered to the trolley she would whine and lunge forward every time a shot was taken, which was rather off-putting for anyone standing nearby. She was extremely keen to get on with the walk and became even more agitated if ever I had to take more than one shot from any particular place. Thankfully she was relatively quiet around the greens unless one ended up in a bunker, when she again tended to become rather impatient.

Visits to the Isle of Wight

The accompanying photograph shows Benji and Poppi patiently waiting to go for a walk, outside my favourite B&B on the Isle of Wight, the 'Braemar', Grange Road, Shanklin, which lies within fifty yards of the main street which passes through Shanklin Old Village, where there are several picturesque pubs, plus a variety of restaurants and a chip shop. There were also two parks within easy reach.

Poppi stayed there numerous times during her lifetime, as the Isle of Wight became a regular destination for the W.P.C.C. tourists. On a couple of those tours most of the party stayed at the 'Braemar,' until they decided that the night-life was probably more exciting in Ryde. I, however, was more than happy to enjoy the quiet life.

Being a creature of habit, we always stayed in the same small room at the 'Braemar', which had the benefit of being on the ground floor, which meant that we could slip in and out of the house without causing too much disturbance. This was particularly important as we usually went for our first walk of the day at about 6.00 a.m. whilst most of the residents were still asleep. At that time in the morning, we always walked to the Big Mead Recreation Ground, where the dogs chased a ball before we went to the newsagent's shop in the village and bought a copy of 'The Times'. When we returned the dogs would be fed and I would try to do a Sudoku before my predictably boring breakfast of cornflakes followed by scrambled eggs on toast.

As the cricket matches never started before 2 p.m. one could usually visit anywhere upon the Island and get to the match on time. Again, being a creature of habit, I tended to visit the same places year after year, such as Appuldurcombe House, Carisbrooke Castle and Tennyson Down.

The photograph on the right shows Poppi and Benji close to the Needles, having walked over two miles along the West High Down from the National Trust carpark near Nodewell Farm.

Following our brief rest at the Needles we then descended the steep path to the gun emplacement at the Old Battery (on the left), where refreshments were available for both man and dogs, before making the long trek over the Downs back to the car park near the Tennyson Monument. A round trip of about five miles was quite impressive for fourteen year old Benji.

Most afternoons on tour I was usually involved in a cricket match, either as a player or as a scorer. I would try if possible to tether Poppi and Benji together in the shade with a non-spill water bowl in close proximity. They were never any trouble and would lie there patiently waiting for the tea interval when they might possibly manage to scrounge a crumb or two.

On several occasions, particularly if I was scoring, I would look up from my book and see members of the team walking around the boundary with my dogs in tow. Poppi, a supposedly aggressive dog, was quite happy walking with almost complete strangers. It was almost as though Benji had had a calming influence upon her and had explained that those dressed in white were friends.

After the matches ended, whilst the youngsters went out to night clubs and bars I tended to return to the 'Braemar' and a portion of fish and chips from the local chippie, although occasionally I made it back in time to attend the Pensioners' Buffet at the Holliers Inn. The final walk of the day was usually taken through Tower Gardens and down the steep steps to the beach, and then back to the B&B by 10 p.m. before retiring for the night. Boring? Perhaps!

The photograph on the right shows Benji and a muzzled Poppi on the ferry home from the Isle of Wight. As the journey takes only about forty minutes we were sometimes advised to leave the dogs in the car. When they were allowed on board they always had to travel on the top deck.

Benji and Poppi visit Les Vercors 2012

Within six weeks of acquiring Poppi, in March 2012, I started the process of obtaining Poppi a European Union Pet Passport, by having her inoculated against rabies. The photograph on the right was taken specifically to be added to her passport in September, when she had been with us for seven months. By that stage she looked much more confident than when I had first met her and she had really bonded with Benji.

Three days after the cricket season ended, on October 3rd, Poppi boarded a cross channel ferry for the first time, accompanied by that seasoned traveller, Benji, and myself. The first two nights were spent in our usual haunts at Lacre and Dissay-sous-Courcillon whilst on the third evening we booked into an Ibis at Bellerive-sur-Allier near Vichy, before arriving at the chalet in St. Andeol as the sun went down on Saturday evening.

Unfortunately there had been a mix up in my communication with Jolyon as neither he nor Corinne were around, which meant that I seemed doomed to spend the night in the car with the dogs, as it was impossible to gain access to the chalet. I spent the final hour of daylight feeding the dogs and myself, before deciding at 7 o'clock, when it was totally dark that, as there was nothing better to do, I might as well try to get some sleep.

Wrapping myself in my sleeping bag I tried to find some comfort lying across the back seat of the car, with both dogs in the front. That was impossible, however, as the ridge down the centre of the seat dug into my back. The front passenger seat in a reclined position, with my legs on the dashboard, was no better. Just when I had resigned myself to the fact that I would have to spend twelve hours of tossing and turning and failing to find any relief, there came a knock on the window, accompanied by a beam of light from a torch, which drove the dogs mad.

It was rather a scary moment as I could see nothing apart from the glare of the torch. Was it a mass murderer, the police or a friend? Thankfully it was the latter, Jacques from the nearest chalet stood there and invited me to have a meal with Monique and himself and to spend the night in their spare room. What a relief!

After that the holiday proceeded in the same vein as the previous two holidays in the Alps with Jolyon and Corinne visiting at weekends. Although Corinne was more of a cat person and occasionally brought her cat to the chalet in a cage, Jolyon was definitely a dog lover and was constantly the target of Poppi's attention.

The picture on the right shows Jolyon on the patio at the rear of the chalet teasing Poppi with a ball whilst an elderly Benji watches on with interest. Although it is not a great photograph of the dogs, it does amply show the steep slope of the garden with the Alps in the distance. The garden, which had numerous conifers, was over a hundred yards in length and was a nightmare to mow.

One of the most memorable incidents which occurred that holiday involved the totally unpredictable Poppi, a dog whom I would never try to manhandle. To be honest I was basically scared of her. One weekend when Jolyon and Corinne were at the chalet, nosy Poppi decided that she would like to see their bedroom which was accessed by a very steep pine staircase. She climbed up the staircase tentatively with her paws slipping on every pine step, but was then too scared to descend. Jolyon, without a thought for his own safety, grabbed hold of her, put her under his arm and carried her down, without being bitten. I was gobsmacked yet again by her behaviour.

After our hosts returned to Grenoble on Sunday evenings, much of my time was spent doing the same mundane tasks such as washing, cooking and general housework that I did in Cheam; only the view from the window was of beautiful snow capped mountains! We were almost living in splendid isolation as the nearest chalet was over two hundred yards away, and on average a car passed by every ten minutes. I did, however, tend to drive almost every day into Monestier-de-Clermont to buy fresh bread, fruit, vegetables, meat and a three day old copy of any English newspaper that I could find. I was desperate to find out what was going on in Blighty.

Poppi loved the large wooded garden which surrounded the chalet, where she could run around with sticks of varying size, or chase the golf balls that I hit with a wedge, which was the only club that I had taken with me. The photograph on the right shows a rather defensive looking Poppi standing, upon the wooden floor, in the doorway of the chalet with a tired looking Benji lying behind her.

Benji spent most of the holiday ambling slowly around after Poppi, or just chilled out. The photograph on the right shows Benji resting next to Poppi in the long grass above the chalet, whilst the one on the left shows him lying on the wooden floor

next to the unlit stone-built fireplace. It was a place that Poppi, like Gemma before her, avoided like the plague when the fire was lit, as it was forever crackling and occasionally spewing out sprays of sparks. Despite the fact that the fire was surrounded by a large metal fire-guard, the fact that the chalet was constructed entirely of wood meant that one had to be ultra-vigilant whenever the fire was lit.

Although I allowed Poppi and Benji to run freely around the house and garden, I usually found that it was preferable when walking through the wooded slopes of Les Vercors to keep both dogs on their leads. Apart from the dangerous steep-sided gulleys which appeared occasionally, Benji was relatively deaf and might not be able to hear me calling him, whilst Poppi would try to flee whenever she heard a shot being fired by the many heavily armed hunters who would occasionally emerge from the trees. Poppi did not seem to care much for the large hounds who accompanied 'les chasseurs' either.

The most interesting, worrying, and quite costly event of that whole holiday was when Benji got a tick embedded in one of his beautiful sandy coloured eyebrows, probably from lying in the long grass in the photograph above. Monique helped me to telephone a vet in Vif which was about 15 miles away. The journey was along a rather hazardous, twisting, hairpin riddled mountainous road. The vet safely removed the tick, applied Frontline to the dogs, and gave Benji some cortanmycetine cream to be applied to the spot twice a day. The cost of the treatment was 71 Euros, but at least I discovered a small laundrette which I visited the following week much to the amusement of the other customers, as I struggled with the machines.

TIP NUMBER 27: A small plastic tick removing tool which costs less than £3 could save you an expensive vet's bill.

Our departure from St. Andeol was forced upon me by a sudden and unexpected turn of events. On our third weekend at the chalet, Jolyon and Corinne had arrived as usual on the Friday evening, and we spent a very pleasant evening wining and dining in the chalet of Jacques and Monique. The following day, however, it began to snow heavily and, as we sat in the warmth of the living room, we watched the snow gradually deepen on the balcony. Poppi loved the snow although it did make running around with a long stick a little more awkward.

When over sixty centimetres of snow fell in the space of twenty-four hours I began to panic. I could see us being trapped upon the mountain for the whole of the winter as none of the locals could remember such a severe event occurring before the end of October. Although snowploughs worked throughout Saturday night to make the roads passable, it took us at least two hours of hard work on Sunday morning to clear two feet of snow from Jolyon's long driveway, before we escaped off the mountain.

We fled in record time, for me, via Bourges to the gite of Madame Fourdinier where I spent six miserable days watching the rain beating against the windows. During that

time the dogs were basically confined to the farmhouse and were only let outside to go to the toilet. On the seventh day, however, the sun shone and we made our way to Montreuil-sur-Mer where we walked three kilometres around the battlements of the fortress. The photograph on the left was taken early that morning as I walked the dogs to the end of Madame Fourdinier's drive. Poppi was wisely letting Benji stand closest to the goats.

On November 5th we had to make the rather nerve-racking journey to Calais to see Dr. Nowosad, a vet whom Benji had seen in 2010, to have them wormed and to check that they were both in a good enough condition to travel. Poppi was, of course, muzzled because of her aversion to members of the veterinarian profession. I was more than a little worried, however, when Dr. Nowosad insisted that I had to take her muzzle off. He then put his face close to her, whispered in her ear and let her lick him. What he said to her was a mystery but it certainly worked as she made no attempt to bite him, as she again demonstrated her rather unpredictable nature.

Benji, the End of an Era

Despite having promised Jolyon that I would return with the dogs the following year, I had a sinking feeling that Benji might no longer be around as he was already fourteen years old.

Outwardly Benji still looked to be extremely fit. His shiny black coat, with hardly a trace of grey, was in great condition, whilst his symmetrical facial markings were perfect, as were the sandy coloured bushy eye-brows and the still clear brown eyes. Mentally he was still very alert and loved playing with a ball or chewing a bone or his fleece. He would regularly deposit his half chewed bone in my lap, quite confident in the knowledge that I would not keep it. When Gemma and Benji had been puppies I had regularly pretended to eat their food or chew their bones, which meant that they were very relaxed and not at all aggressive where food was concerned.

It was, however, noticeable that Benji was struggling a little with his mobility. He would mount the stairs extremely slowly and struggled to climb into the light blue Hyundai i30, in which we had travelled to France. Unlike my other cars the i30 still had all its seats intact. This led to me buying a foldable wooden ramp which can be seen in the accompanying photograph. I must admit that Benji was rather reluctant to use it and had to be enticed into the car with a treat or two.

In the middle of January 2013, Cheam experienced one of those brief snow showers which covered the park and garden in a thin coating of soft fluffy whiteness, which lasted for just over twenty four hours, before it turned to slush. The park became a magical wonderland with groups of excitable youngsters pulling sledges and building snowmen.

The photograph on the right shows Poppi revelling in pushing an old punctured football through the snow in the garden, whilst a seemingly relaxed Benji looked on. The photograph on the left shows them a short time afterwards when their paws

had been dried, and they were waiting patiently in the conservatory before they were allowed to enter the house. Benji looked to be in excellent condition with his beautiful brown eyes and his smooth lustrous coat. It was hard to think that he was almost fifteen years old.

In February and March Benji had several bouts of colitis. Initially I tried to cure him with a few doses of old fashion kaolin and morphine but, when this treatment failed, I had to bite the bullet and make an appointment with the Vet, who not only treated the colitis with anti-biotics but discovered that his heart problem had deteriorated. As a result Benji found himself on a very bland diet of scrambled egg, rice and chicken, with Vetmedin tablets added to his daily dose of Enacard tablets.

By April, although Benji looked quite fit despite losing a little weight, it was obvious that he was struggling to digest his food and he seemed reluctant to eat. Famotidine tablets, which alleviate some stomach problems and Cerenia (anti-nausea) tablets were added to his daily medication.

I spent much of my time cooking rice, fish, chicken and scrambled eggs, which I then tried to force feed him by prizing his jaws apart to spoon the food into his mouth. I then clamped his mouth shut until he swallowed the food. It was quite a time consuming process but at least I felt that I was trying to help him. Sadly, however, his condition did not appear to improve.

Following an X-ray and urine tests it was decided to perform an exploratory laparotomy on him on Friday April 19th. The previous day he had been playing with me quite happily in the garden heading a football back to me. Both of us were oblivious as to what was to happen the following day.

That night Benji was starved of all food and was taken to the Wingrave Hospital at about 8 o'clock the following morning. When Aaron Ruck, the vet, collected him from the waiting room, Benji went off with him quite happily and never even looked back at either Poppi or myself. He had had numerous visits to the vets in his lifetime and was quite used to being taken into the operating room after all.

At 12.30, whilst I was making a bite to eat, the phone rang and it was Aaron with the sad news that the laparotomy had revealed that there was cancer on two of his internal organs and that it was impossible to operate on both of them. He wanted to know what I wanted to do. Eventually we decided that it was probably for the best that he was not revived after the operation.

Within the hour, I put on a brave face and collected Benji's lifeless body that was still warm to the touch. It was hard to believe that he was dead as he looked so peaceful. When I arrived home I gently placed his body upon the floor of the conservatory so that Poppi could understand that her friend was dead.

That weekend I made myself unavailable for cricket and took him to the paddock at Oakwood Hill where he was buried with some of his favourite toys, next to his sister Gemma. It is a little poignant to think that one of my last memories of him had been of him walking casually through a flock of my cousin's chickens in that same paddock, less than a month before his death.

It was the end of an era! I had been heart-broken when Ben died and had tried to replace him with two puppies from the same kennels, in order to keep his memory alive. Now all connection with Ben had been severed. In the space of sixteen months I had lost two marvellous friends, who seemed to be loved by everyone they met. I had witnessed every moment of their lives as they progressed from puppyhood, through adolescence to adulthood.

Although Gemma was an affectionate and gentle dog, Benji was special as he had replaced Ben in my heart. He was such a placid, kind soul who seemed to understand my every thought and action. I must admit that I felt a pang of anger to think that he

had walked blithely to his death with Arran, without a backward glance, as though he had never really cared for me. I was desolate to think that I had never had the opportunity to say a proper farewell to him, although it was some consolation to think that he appeared to be quite happy the last time that I saw him, and that he was spared any future suffering.

Despite the fact that both Benji and Gemma passed away over a decade ago, they are regularly mentioned by my friends. Recently Rob Waite, a fellow Worcester Park cricketer, sent me the following two photographs that he took on tour in either Devon or on the Isle of Wight. The photograph on the left reminds me of just how tolerant and popular Benji was. Unlike Poppi he would never have bitten anyone.

In that photograph he was being manhandled by James Cameron to look at the camera. If one looks very closely at the photograph one can see Gemma's nose and legs behind the bench, keeping a safe distant from James's attention.

The photograph on the right shows them in their usual habitat at a cricket match: tethered to a bench in the shade with their non-spill water bowl, which figures in several photographs, in close proximity.

———————

Poppi and Sophie

Another reason that I was angry with Benji for dying was the fact that he had left me with his supposed companion, Poppi, a dog with whom it is fair to say that I had not bonded. Whereas I had acquired all my other Border Collies as puppies and felt extremely comfortable handling them, Poppi was already three and a half years old when she entered my life and I was extremely wary of laying hands upon her. She was not a dog whom I would have dared cuddle.

Although Poppi had not bonded with me, she had formed a strong relationship with Benji who was the only dog that she had really known. She was noticeably devastated

by his death and spent much of her time lying listlessly upon her bed in the spare room or behind the front door.

Whether Benji had appreciated it or not, Poppi had tended to follow him everywhere, loved playing with him and was forever trying to dominate him. Following the trauma that she had experienced the previous year of being forcibly removed from the family that she loved, now her best friend was dead.

My method of coping with Benji's death was to flee from the scene of the crime. Benji had died on Friday, was buried on Saturday and I drove 250 miles north to stay with my brother, Bill, in Darwen for a few days on the Sunday. There poor Poppi was confined to my bedroom as Nelson, the tiny black Labrador, was very territorial. Poppi in her turn seemed to be adverse to black Labradors. It had been, after all, because of her altercation with a couple of black Labradors that she had been expelled from the agility course.

We did take the dogs a couple of walks in Boldventure Park where there was an uneasy truce between them. The photograph on the right is another one that was taken

in Marsden Park in Nelson during that visit and shows Poppi playing with another large stick, having forgotten for a short time the death of her best friend.

When we returned to Cheam, my method of coping with Benji's death was to throw myself into my sport. That summer of 2013 I played 42 games of cricket for Worcester Park and Surrey Seniors. As the Captain of the Sunday Social team, the Midweek team and the Fourth XI League team I had to organise approximately 60 teams that season which kept me fully occupied. I probably sent over a thousand texts and emails, made numerous phone calls, and entered all the match results on the Playcricket website.

I also played golf two or three times a week with J.J.M. at Cuddington. Although Poppi usually accompanied me whenever I played golf, she had to be left at home whenever I played cricket at Worcester Park because of their discriminatory stance against allowing dogs to attend matches. I must admit, however, that I felt bad whenever I had to leave her at home, but cricket came first.

During the Sixties I had become addicted to playing bridge in the sixth form at Nelson Grammar School and at the College of St. Mark and St. John, Chelsea. For the whole 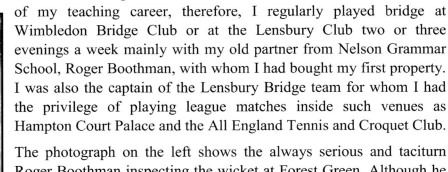 of my teaching career, therefore, I regularly played bridge at Wimbledon Bridge Club or at the Lensbury Club two or three evenings a week mainly with my old partner from Nelson Grammar School, Roger Boothman, with whom I had bought my first property. I was also the captain of the Lensbury Bridge team for whom I had the privilege of playing league matches inside such venues as Hampton Court Palace and the All England Tennis and Croquet Club.

The photograph on the left shows the always serious and taciturn Roger Boothman inspecting the wicket at Forest Green. Although he always made a fuss of my dogs he was basically a cat man.

As I also played bridge regularly with my golfing partner and work colleague, John Murtagh, at the Belmont and Chipstead clubs, I spent many evenings away from home during the lifetime of Ben, Benji and Gemma. It was, therefore, a blessing to have had some great long time lodgers such as Denise Tierney, Colin Ritchie, Margaret Tetlow and Suzi Stuttard, which meant that my dogs were rarely left at home alone.

By 2006, however, I had given up playing bridge as I preferred to spend my evenings resting in front of the television, rather than trying to explain to an overweight opponent what I understood by my partner's bid, when all I wanted to do was to go to bed. Apart from attending an horology course on Fridays in the winter, therefore, I rarely left the house in the evenings. Life, therefore, was not very stimulating for Poppi as all her master did was watch television, work on his computer or read. But at least I was there!

Although I did not neglect Poppi physically and made sure that she was well fed and had plenty of exercise, I was acutely aware that she was not being stretched mentally or socially. As she had been banned from the agility class her interaction with other dogs had been severely curtailed, as had a great avenue of mental stimulation.

I did try to play ball with Poppi as often as possible around the house or in the garden that summer, and occasionally set up the cheap plastic agility equipment in the park. In the winter, however, any activity outside the house became less frequent as I was reluctant to let Poppi get muddy as she was a nightmare to clean. As a result I decided that the only option was to try to find a companion dog for the companion dog, and so I began to look again at the Border Collie Trust's website.

Discovering Sophie

On Saturday December 14th, 2013 I decided to call in unannounced on the Border Collie Trust's H.Q. in Colton, Rugeley on my journey North to deliver Christmas presents to my brother and all his family. When I arrived mid-afternoon there was a tiny nine week old Border Collie Cross puppy called Sophie scampering around the reception area, chasing an equally tiny kitten who kept jumping on chairs and teasing the puppy. Although she was described as being a 'Cross breed' she had all the typical markings of a pure Border Collie.

The photograph on the right was Sophie's mug-shot from the Border Collie Rescue's files. The number was her reference number, not the year.

Sophie was one of a litter of six who had arrived from a rescue in Ireland the previous day. They were all microchipped, wormed and inoculated upon arrival and were all given names beginning with the letter 'S'. Unfortunately, as I was unable to see the rest of the litter and as I had wanted a boy, I decided to carry on with my journey.

Whilst driving North, however, I could not stop thinking of that captivating little puppy who had been running around the reception area. It had obviously been love at first sight. As a result I pulled into the first service area that I came across and rang up the Rescue and told them that I would like to re-home Sophie if that were possible, and would be passing through Rugeley the following Tuesday on my return home. I was extremely pleased when they promised to reserve her for me.

That evening as I sat watching Strictly Come Dancing, a programme that I had rarely watched, with June, my sister-in-law, I received a sign that Sophie was the dog for me when I saw that one of the competitors was also called Sophie, the singer-song writer Sophie Ellis-Bextor.

On the Tuesday morning I drove back to the Border Collie Trust and walked Poppi around the grounds and into the reception area, where I wanted to introduce her to her new housemate and to let the staff see that, despite Poppi's problems, I had taken good care of her and could be trusted to look after Sophie. I must admit that the first meeting was not auspicious and so I returned Poppi to the car. I wondered if she remembered her short time at the centre. Perhaps she even thought that I was taking her back home or returning her to the Centre.

After passing the interview, filling in the necessary forms and promising to have her neutered the following year, I paid the £150 re-homing fee. I was also given details of the injections which Sophie had had and was told that she was known to be suffering from or could be incubating kennel cough. Fortunately the cough never transpired.

It is probably not surprising to note that as Sophie was only nine weeks old, she was colour coded 'Green'. In a way that was a great responsibility for me. How she developed was entirely in my hands. If she were rehomed now she is over ten years old, I would hope that she might still be considered to be worthy of a green code, as she loves everybody and is quite good in the company of other dogs.

After we left the Centre I placed the little dog into a small box in the open luggage area of the Hyundai i40 with Poppi lying quietly, harnessed in place upon the back seat of the car, and drove as quickly as possible the 150 miles home.

When we arrived home I let the little dog into the garden for a short time so that she could go to the toilet. I tried again to introduce her to Poppi who made it obvious that she did not like the intruder and kept lunging at her, although I kept her on a very tight lead. The fact that Sophie rolled over on her back, with her paws in the air, in a gesture of submission did not really seem to have much affect upon Poppi.

TIP NUMBER 29: It is best to introduce the new dog to the existing dog in the garden rather than in the home as the old dog might be very territorial.

House training Sophie

Poppi's rather aggressive attitude meant that it was imperative that I kept the dogs apart. As a result Sophie spent most of her time in the kitchen, which has a three foot high sliding wooden barrier in place to separate it from the dining room. The photograph on the right shows Sophie at 6.15 p.m. on December 17th, 2013, on a nice clean carpet following her first meal in her new home. She had just been taken to the toilet in the garden.

Sophie was the easiest of my four puppies to house train, probably because I could spend a lot of time with her. When I had first acquired Ben, Benji and Gemma I was still working. I was well aware of when she might want to go to the toilet and either placed her upon a newspaper in the corner of the kitchen or took her into the garden.

TIP NUMBER 30: Puppies usually need to go to the toilet after food, sleep, play and excitement.

Fortunately there were very few toilet accidents in the house and they were quickly mopped up and the area was doused with white vinegar. What did worry me, however, was her propensity to try to chew everything with her needle sharp tiny teeth. The T.V. stand, the side board and the kitchen carpet all bear signs of her handiwork. Whenever I caught her nibbling on wood or fabric I tried to turn her attention to either a hefty cooked bone or to one of her toys. My main cause of concern was that she might try to bite one of the electric cables which littered the floor of the living room.

TIP NUMBER 31: Do NOT use bleach based cleaners if there is a house training accident. It is better to use white vinegar or a non-biological cleaner.

As Sophie had to be fed about four times a day for the first four months, it made sense

to keep her near the source of her food in the kitchen, where she could be protected from the teeth of her wicked step mother behind the sliding barrier.

The photo on the right shows Sophie on that first evening in Netley Close. She was gently nibbling on a soft fabric Father Christmas with an empty food dish behind her.

TIP NUMBER 32: It is best to feed a new puppy away from an existing dog, preferably in another room. Later one can gradually move them together.

Sophie seemed to be perfectly happy whilst I remained in the kitchen, but whenever I left the room she would yap and throw herself at the wooden barrier in an effort to jump over it. As a result I transferred one of the cages from the conservatory to the living room and placed it on the corner of the couch. It was supposed to be only a temporary measure but it remained there for nine years.

Having a large cage on the settee did nothing to enhance the ambience of the room but, as I no longer had any lodgers, and, as visitors were few and far between, it served a useful function. Over the following nine years, therefore, whenever Sophie felt tired and fancied a rest, or when she wanted to escape Poppi's unwanted attention, she would nudge the door open, and escape to her own safe place.

For the first few days at Chez Stemp, however, Sophie needed a really safe place as Poppi was not a happy dog, as she seemed intent upon attacking the intruder. Whenever I wanted to let Sophie out of the cage to play in the living room, Poppi had to be tethered to the heavy side board.

I must admit that there were several occasions in the first ten days when I doubted the wisdom of having obtained a new dog, as Poppi continually lunged at her. Every day, therefore, for an increasing amount of time, I would try to initiate close contact between the two dogs. I would put Poppi on a very short lead in the living room and encourage the little one to approach her. Sophie, for her part, wanted to be friends. She would wag her tail gently and would lie on her back in submission before a seemingly aggressive Poppi. Gradually, however, the aggression waned and after a fortnight I felt confident enough to let Poppi off the lead in the company of the little dog.

Eventually Poppi's distrust of Sophie seemed to subside completely, and it was almost as though a well-hidden maternal gene rose to the surface. I think that the best example of this occurred after Sophie had been with us for five weeks and I took her for her first walk into Cheam Village. On that occasion I tethered them both to a bicycle rack outside Boots. From inside the shop I saw a lady approach the dogs with the obvious intention of making a fuss of Sophie. As I was not there Poppi obviously thought that she was responsible for Sophie and, as she was unaware of the stranger's intention, she made it very clear that her attention was unwanted. That was the only time that I ever saw Poppi bare her teeth at a lady, although she had apparently bitten a couple of women whilst with her previous family.

The photograph above shows the tiny, fluffy fourteen week old puppy waiting to go on her first walk into the Village. They looked very relaxed and calm in each other's company, as though they were mother and daughter.

The photograph on the left shows a rather haughty looking Poppi with her front left paw raised. It looks as though she is about to tap Sophie on her bottom to make her sit down.

The photograph on the following page was taken on the same day in 'The Prince of Wales' pub. It was Sophie's first ever visit to a pub. Poppi knew that if she stared at the barmaid for long enough, Ronnie, would give them a treat. Although it is a rather dark photograph it is another example of how comfortable the duo appeared to be together. Poppi was no longer pining for Benji, but had a new friend in her life. Sophie in her turn seemed to have adopted Poppi as her mother.

Pre-Covid we used to regularly visit the pub after shopping in the Village, and it used to amuse passers-by to witness the dogs dragging me up the steps of the pub and through the swinging front door. Sophie quickly began to associate 'The Prince of Wales' with treats, and although it is a couple of years since I last had a drink in the pub, she still tries to pull me inside whenever we pass the entrance.

As the 'Little Un', as I called her, became more confident, she spent much of her time either following Poppi around the house or just watching her. She seemed fascinated by Poppi, whom it was difficult to ignore.

Much of the dogs' time together was devoted to play-fighting, as Poppi tried to prepare Sophie for life in the real world. She would lie passively upon her bed whilst Sophie would circle her, then attack and try and bite Poppi before retreating, only to attack again from a different direction. The photograph on the right shows their teeth clashing in one of those attacks.

These fights tended to terminate whenever the needle sharp teeth of the puppy caused Poppi genuine pain and she reverted to type. Whenever that happened, Sophie, as she was that small, had the ability to hide under almost every piece of furniture in the living room. I have a vivid memory of an angry Poppi trying to fish Sophie out from under the sideboard with her paws, and failing.

Even today Sophie has a penchant for lying in enclosed spaces, which is probably a throw back to her early days of hiding from Poppi. In the garden one of her favourite defensive positions can be seen in the photograph on the right. It was the stone bench under the Lleylandii trees which I lined with artificial grass to keep her clean.

One of Sophie's most annoying habits is her ability to hide in the circular base of my recliner chair, which is only eight inches high. Apart from the scratches to the wood work, it made moving the chair either backwards or forwards almost impossible. It was, however, relatively difficult for Poppi to attack her there, as Sophie could hide her head behind the reclining foot rest.

Another of Sophie's favourite hiding places was under the sheet covered wicker-work furniture in the conservatory. Lying there protected her not only from Poppi but provided shade from temperatures which regularly topped 100^0F in the summer. She usually stayed in the conservatory whenever Poppi and I were playing ball games in the garden.

Sophie actually seems relatively oblivious to extreme temperatures as on the coldest winter day she can often be found asleep on one of the chairs in the conservatory.

Sophie goes to the toilet

Shortly before I acquired Sophie I had spent a lot of time and money trying to improve the garden by returfing the lawn and replacing the old shed and the fence, both of which were 35 years old. The photograph on the right shows Sophie when she was about three months old sitting on part of the lawn, besides the shed with the pristine new fence behind her.

Sadly I discovered that letting two bitches loose in the garden was a recipe for disaster. They quickly ruined the lawn, as wherever they squatted to urinate, the grass became 'burned' or 'scorched' due to the excess nitrogen in their urine. Although I tried to hose down any spot where they had urinated, I realised that I was fighting a losing cause. As a result, six months later, all the grass was ripped up and replaced by a beautiful, but expensive (£1,700), green carpet, where the dogs could wee without leaving any unsightly brown patches behind.

Another benefit of the artificial grass was that it made it easier to spot where Sophie had poo-ed, as it quickly became obvious that she was a 'walker'. The photograph on

the left shows an ungainly looking Sophie on one of these walks. Ten years later she is still a walker.

When Sophie was very young she would often hare around the trees and the garden a couple of times, as though it were a race track, before coming to a sudden halt and assuming a crouched position.

Usually when she wants to poo she starts off on the grass under the Lleylandi trees on the left of the garden and wanders around in front of the trees to the path on the right of the lawn where she tends to stop, Occasionally she will walk around the back of the trees and start again. Sometimes she might walk twenty or thirty yards in total and can leave up to twenty tiny deposits.

To gather up the poo in the garden is extremely easy. I use a couple of old trowels to scoop it up and put it in the bin. I quickly found out in the park, however, that it was extremely difficult to pick up all the poo of a walker, and, as a result, I never let her wander freely but keep her on a lead, when she is not chasing a ball, as she rarely tries to poo whilst on the lead. Whenever we go to a cricket match or play a round of golf, I always make sure that I have 'emptied her' before I go out. I merely say, "Sophie, do poo," and she usually performs as required.

TIP NUMBER 33: It might be best to seek the advice of a vet if your dog walks and poos as it might indicate a problem. With Sophie it is just an annoying habit.

Socialising Sophie

As an extremely tiny, beautifully marked Border Collie, Sophie was immediately very popular with everyone she met. Whenever we went for a walk complete strangers would approach us and make a fuss of her. Sophie, in her turn, would try to make eye contact and wag her tail vigorously whenever we passed anyone, and unless I kept a tight hold of her she would embarrass me by jumping up at them, so that they could stroke her. Even today she loves nothing more than being loved by anyone we meet, and still embarrasses me by jumping up at them, particularly at the golf club. Although I always apologise for her behaviour, most of the members tell me not to worry and reward Sophie by making a fuss of her. I can't win!

What really surprised me on our first few ventures into the park, however, was that Sophie, although she seemed perfectly confident in Poppi's company, she appeared to be scared of other dogs. On one occasion she literally screamed in terror as a large dog approached her. I had never heard a dog scream before! That was when I decided that I must make a positive effort to try to socialise her with other dogs, and so, when she was five months old in March 2014, I enrolled her upon a Puppy Training Course at Headley with CK9 Training and Poppi's old friend, Chantal Karyta (Catherine).

Although all the puppies on the course were lovely, I liked to think that my tiny black and white Border Collie was the star of the show. She passed the course with flying colours and her certificate still adorns the fridge. More important than the training, however, was the fact that, after a tentative start, Sophie gradually became confident around the other puppies on the course. Poppi, in the meantime, was quite happy sleeping on the back seat of the car.

Sophie and Agility

As Chantal thought that Sophie would be good at agility when she was a little older, we spent an hour almost every Wednesday morning over the next three years, with a small group of fellow dog owners, with dogs ranging in size from squat French Bulldogs to long-legged, ungainly Labradoodles, in a variety of small fields between Brockham and Banstead doing agility. Poppi, of course, looked after the car.

What all those venues had in common was the fact that they tended to be exposed to the vagaries of the weather, which often meant that Sophie tended to end up coated in mud. On other occasions, however, the sun beat down upon us and one had to find shelter wherever possible. In the photograph on the right Sophie was sheltering from the sun with a tiny Terrier in the shadow beneath the A-frame.

Sophie would have been much more successful at agility if she had had a younger, more nimble owner. As it was, she was very quick and enthusiastic but rarely went the right way around the course, which provided the other dog owners with plenty of laughs. The photographs below show a seventy year old owner trying to keep up with a young Border Collie as she tackled a weave and crossed the four foot high dog-walk.

Sophie really loved the agility course and would bark excitedly as she jumped the hurdles, or sped along the top of the dog walk. Her main problem was that she was too quick and would often try to cut corners: she would also often miss a couple of poles at the end of the weave, or she would jump off the A-frame and the dog-walk before she reached the end of the obstacle, for which points would have been deducted.

The only piece of apparatus with which Sophie had a real problem was the see-saw. She would walk tentatively up it, but as soon as it reached the horizontal and started to tip over, she would usually jump off.

She absolutely loved the A-frame and would often sit on it at head height, as it gave her a better view of what was happening, and allowed her to make easy eye contact with her owner.

The tunnel was also a piece of useful equipment in Sophie's mind as it was a great place in which to shelter on a hot day.

Chantal would occasionally use one of her Shelties to demonstrate how one should control ones dog. She made it look extremely easy! The photograph on the left shows Chantal with her red Border Collie and three beautiful, prize-winning Shelties, one of whom can be seen, on YouTube, taking part in an agility final at Crufts in 2016.

Each Christmas after the final agility session of the season, all the class and their hounds would descend upon a local, dog-friendly pub, such as 'The Cock' at Headley. It was quite a chaotic gathering with six or seven humans and about ten dogs, although Poppi, unsurprisingly, was not invited and had to remain in the car park.

In order to try to improve our performances I regularly used to take Sophie onto the Rec. in front of my house and set up a small agility course which usually had a ten pole weave, three or four jumps, a hoop and a canvas tunnel. As a treat for completing the course, I would throw a ball for her to chase. The photograph on the right is a rare one as it shows Sophie sitting besides the first pole of the weave. It was difficult to get her to sit besides the weave as she was that keen to demonstrate her prowess (or not) that she usually started before I gave her the command, "Weave!"

We certainly attracted quite a lot of attention mainly from dog-walkers, and on more than one occasion even received a slight ripple of applause. Less welcome, however, was the attention from some of the dogs being walked, who obviously thought it was a great game to chase Sophie. Poppi did not help the situation either as she barked continually if tethered to a bollard and, if allowed to wander freely, she would often stand besides the weave or knock over the fences thereby impeding Sophie's progress, as appears evident from the photograph on the right.

When Chantal moved to South Africa our weekly agility classes ended, as did my motivation to carry on training Sophie at home, as I found that it was quite time consuming carrying all my equipment on to the Rec. and setting it up. Our sessions, therefore, became fewer as the years passed. I must admit that I feel guilty about depriving Sophie of the opportunity of doing something that she really enjoyed.

Even though I am now too lazy to set up my equipment in the park, I still try to encourage Sophie to be agile whenever possible. Quite often we visit the Outdoor Gym equipment at the top of the Rec. where I encourage Sophie to jump over the wooden balance in a figure of eight motion. On one occasion I heard a passing youngster say, "That's sick!" which I think meant that he was impressed.

Several times a year we visit Ewhurst in the hope that Rosemary has an agility course set up in the paddock next to her house for her latest Border Collie, Zack, who is pictured looking over the garden fence in 2018. As Rosemary is now in her eighties agility tends to be a summer only activity.

The two photographs below show that, although Sophie is no longer a youngster and has not had a proper lesson for years, she still loves to race around an agility course and is an excellent jumper. If one looks carefully one can see an aged Poppi watching on in the distance.

Sophie's Lineage

As strangers were forever enquiring as to whether Sophie was a Border Collie as she was so small, I decided to have her DNA tested in 2016. Wisdom Panel sent me the following information on July 25th, 2016, which shows that, although Sophie is a cross breed, she is predominantly a Border Collie.

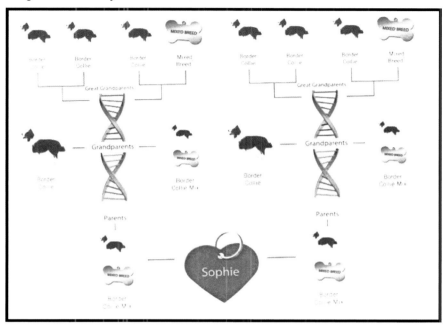

The accompanying information stated that, *'Sophie's DNA sample clusters tightly with the purebred Border Collie cluster'*. Of the other breeds who might have had an influence upon her DNA, the strongest statistical likelihood points towards the Maltese breed, which made a lot of sense when one considers her size. Less likely, but not improbable, were the Shetland Sheepdog, the Golden Retriever, the Australian Koolie and the French Bulldog. Whatever the influence, for me Sophie was my 'Lap-Collie' who always answered to the name 'Little Un'.

Sophie and Poppi at the Vets

I have never seen a dog who loved going to the vets more than Sophie. From her very first visit as a twelve week old puppy to the Wingrave Veterinarian Practice at Court Rec. in Epsom, she loved all the fuss levied upon her by the staff. She quickly realised that if she wagged her tail enough she would be rewarded with a gravy bone not only from the vet and the nurses, but from Pauline in reception.

Whenever we arrived in the car park at the vets, I often let Sophie out of the car first whilst I was putting the lead on Poppi, who was not quite as enthusiastic as her step daughter. Sophie always made a bee-line towards the front door of the practice and waited for me to put a lead upon her. On one occasion, however, finding the outside door open, she ran inside, zoomed around the reception area before making her way back stage to peals of laughter from the nursing staff. As that sort of behaviour was not really encouraged, after that incident I always ensured that she was on the lead if the front door was open.

Whenever we entered the waiting room, I always weighed both dogs before sitting down. The muzzled Poppi would usually sprawl across the floor daring anyone to step on her, whilst Sophie usually sat upright next to me upon a chair as though it was the most natural thing to do. She loved being able to look me closely in the eye. This behaviour again usually engendered a degree of amusement with any client who witnessed her behaviour.

As soon as the surgery door opened and we were beckoned in, usually by Ejaz Hameed, I would let Sophie off the lead. She would race into the room, jump onto a chair and from there onto the examination table, where she would lie in a crouched position, apparently staring at the computer screen. In actuality she was staring at the jar of gravy biscuits next to the monitor. This behaviour, of course, amazed and amused everyone, including the vet, who happened to witness it.

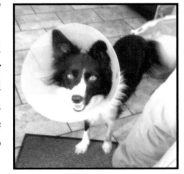

Even after being spayed when she was a year old, and being forced to wear a rather annoying plastic cone, her enthusiasm for visiting the vets has never waned, and although Sophie rarely had any medical issues which necessitated a visit to the vets, Poppi certainly had more than her fair share, which meant that Sophie was able to visit the vets usually two or three times a month.

Although Sophie was a dream patient for the vet, as she allowed him to prod and poke her on the table to his heart's content, Poppi was another matter. Even though she wore a canvas muzzle, a rigid plastic Baskerville mask still had to be worn as well if she were going to be examined, and there was no way that we could place her on the table without a struggle. Ergo she had to be examined on the floor with me tightly holding her harness and muzzle. As soon as the session was over, the muzzles were removed and Poppi reverted, in the hope of getting a treat, to being an exceedingly well behaved dog.

Poppi's behaviour in the consulting room certainly improved over the years as she no longer went completely mad at the sight of a stethoscope. She even allowed the vet to use it on her for three or four seconds before trying to bite him. I think that Sophie's love of being in the room had a calming affect upon Poppi, plus she could watch Sophie being examined and her submissive reaction to it.

TIP NUMBER 33: Separating a dog from the pack and taking it into a strange room can be distressing. If possible take a companion into the consulting room.

Poppi and Sophie on Cricket Tour

Between 2014 and 2021 Poppi, Sophie and myself went on about five cricket tours with Worcester Park C.C. to the Isle of Wight, and each time we stayed in the same small room, on the ground floor of the Braemar Hotel in Shanklin Old Village. Sophie was about nine months old when she went on her first tour. Poppi, however, was an old hand and had done it all before.

The photograph on the right shows the dogs with young Tom Cronk on the top deck of the ferry. Tom, who was a fellow left arm spinner, was a very quiet, responsible lad who had been my passenger on the trip down to Portsmouth. Unfortunately most of the other members of the party, who had booked into the same hotel, were rather lacking in Tom's restrained qualities.

The majority of the party were in their twenties and their idea of a good time was to get up late, have a couple of pints at lunchtime and a bite to eat, followed by a non-too-serious game of cricket. The series of fines imposed upon the players after the match were then followed by more drinks and a visit to the night spots of Sandown. The day usually culminated when the extremely intoxicated and drunken players returned to the hotel in the early hours of the morning.

My idea of a good evening was much more boring. If possible I would patronise the Senior Citizens buffet at the Hollier's Hotel, watch a bit of television and then take the dogs for a final evening stroll around the Shanklin Chine or Tower Gardens. In the morning I would usually visit the Big Mead Rec. at about 6 a.m. to let the dogs chase a ball, before walking into the village to buy a newspaper. This was followed by breakfast which most of my fellow tourists missed as they were still abed, before I visited one of the many marvellous tourist attractions on the island, with the dogs, such as Carisbrooke Castle, before an afternoon of cricket. The photograph above shows the dogs sitting on the stone steps of the castle's battlements.

The photograph on the left shows Sophie being cuddled, or strangled, by our young Australian overseas player, Brenton Deysal, outside a pub before our first match against Arreton. The drink before Brenton certainly did not impair his ability as he scored a fine undefeated century that afternoon.

Sophie was an instant hit with most of the players, and because of her size, was often treated as though she were a rather fluffy 9 kilogram toy. I had to rescue her on more than one occasion when she was being used as an alarm clock by some of the players, who thought that it was highly amusing to drop her onto one of their sleeping

team-mates. The photograph above which was provided by Rob Waite, ten years after the incident, shows Jon Faller-Fritsch appearing to take his rude awakening in good stead. Sophie seemed to think that it was a great game and loved all the attention.

When not abusing Sophie my fellow tourists were sometimes useful as can be seen in the accompanying grainy photograph which shows Matt Probert, Charlie King and Rob Waite walking the dogs around the boundary at Ryde, whilst I was scoring beside the pavilion. Sometimes life on tour could be extremely exhausting and not everyone survived the experience. When we left the

island on the Friday, Matt Probert (on the left of the photograph) was still recovering in a hospital bed from an illness which was probably exacerbated by too many nights spent clubbing.

The Worcester Park cricket tour to the Isle of Wight certainly improved the following year when most of the young tourists decided that they would stay in Ryde as the nightlife was supposedly better there. That decision meant that we tended to get an uninterrupted night's sleep and there was no longer any danger to Sophie.

The most memorable part of the 2015 tour was the fact that two young Indians, Mo Ibrahim and Gurpreet Singh, who played regularly for my Saturday Fourth XI and Sunday Social side, decided that they would like to go on tour, despite the fact that they could not even afford to stay in the cheapest room on the island. Their solution was to borrow a tiny two man tent, which they pitched on a campsite, close to the shoreline near St. Lawrence, Ventnor. The tent can be seen in the photograph on the opposite page.

One could not help but feel sorry for the two lads as, although the campsite had access to running water, there was little else to recommend it, which was probably the reason that they only saw one other tent there that week. There was certainly no nightlife for Mo and Gurpreet as they had no transport, and once the sun had set the only light came from the moon, the stars and a flashlight which I had lent them. Apparently it was quite spooky according to Mo, as all one could hear were the sounds of animals moving around and the lapping of the waves.

As Shanklin was much closer to their campsite than Ryde I became their designated driver, picking them up before matches and dropping them off at the end of the day. That was not great news for Gurpreet as he was one of those sad people who is rather scared of dogs. Mo, on the other hand, was a dog lover as can be seen from the photograph on the right. Even Poppi looked quite happy at being manhandled by Mo who, apart from being

great with the dogs, was an extremely useful medium pace bowler and had the ability to bat both left and right handed.

When the match on Wednesday was cancelled, it was a great opportunity to take Mo and Gurpreet sight seeing. We started at the smallest church on the Island, at St. Lawrence near Ventnor, before moving on to Appuldurcombe House and Carisbrooke Castle. One of the benefits of ferrying the lads around was that I ended up with several photographs of myself with the dogs.

The photograph on the right shows Poppi, Sophie and myself before the Old Church of St. Lawrence. Whilst Poppi looks quite relaxed I was having to hold Sophie with her head facing the camera. Although she is really quite photogenic, if ever she notices anyone trying to take a photograph of her, she always flattens her ears and looks away.

I never featured in any of the matches which were played in 2016 as I was injured, but set myself a goal of trying to photograph a red squirrel. I spent about three days hiking around the western edge of the island where there was a preponderance of road signs warning motorists to beware of Red Squirrels, but to no avail.

On the final morning, whilst walking the dogs close to Shanklin in the Alverston Mead Woodland and Nature Reserve, where I took numerous photographs of long-horned cattle, I eventually managed to snap this photograph of a Red Squirrel nibbling away at a peanut close to one of the hides.

As the years rolled by, my playing participation in the tours lessened, although I did make an appearance at most of the games and occasionally scored. The photograph on the right shows Jon Faller-Fritsch and Sophie intently watching the action on the field at Porchfield in 2017, whilst Poppi was just chilling out.

For me the tour was a chance to really bond with my dogs and to try to thoroughly explore the island. We even made friends with one of the local dog walkers on Big Mead Rec., Graham, who always walked his German Shepherd Skye early every morning. I must admit that I was always worried whenever Skye and Poppi chased a ball that it might end up in a fight. Sophie, however, was far too nimble to be caught by either dog.

One of our most memorable days on the Isle of Wight occurred on our final trip to the Isle of Wight in 2021 when a group of the players and myself decided to play a round of golf at the picturesque Freshwater Bay Golf Club, which seems to be perched precariously on Afton Downs atop of the Freshwater Cliffs and the Military Road.

When we arrived at the Golf Club at about ten o'clock the weather was ideal for golf. The temperature was in the low twenties and there was a gentle cooling breeze emanating from the English Channel. The photograph on the right shows Joe Hill practising his putting before the round began. Beyond him one can see the clear blue sky merging into the darker blue of the ocean. On the fringe of the green both dogs were looking eager to begin their walk. Poppi being a great ball player was looking at the players on the green, despite the fact that her eyesight was extremely poor.

Within an hour of the round beginning there was a sudden change in the weather pattern, as dark clouds rolled across the Downs and the heavens opened. For the next couple of hours we were exposed to a constant downpour and, having left my waterproofs in the car, both dogs and myself were soaked to the skin. I did have the luxury of being able to change my shirt after the round, but the dogs remained damp, and smelly, until late afternoon.

Poppi finally acknowledges her new master

For her first three years at Chez Stemp, Poppi was a fiercely independent character who resented being ordered around and would show her teeth at the drop of a hat. I think that she was still traumatised from having been rejected by her first family and refused to accept me as the leader of the pack.

I like to think that I treated Poppi well. I certainly fed her well and regularly played with her, but one would hardly say that we were close. Perhaps it was my fault as she had to compete for my affection, firstly with Benji and then with a charming puppy. I found some of the things that she did, such as pulling the protective sheets off the furniture in the conservatory or digging in the garden extremely annoying. I was forever telling her off whilst she did not really appear to care what I thought.

Probably the greatest example of her independence was that at night time she preferred to sleep on the small single bed that Denise had used in the spare room, whilst both Benji and Sophie had opted for sleeping in the living room. She did, however, stop rucking up the sheets on that bed after being told off several times. The bed in the downstairs bedroom, however, was still fair game, unless I placed chairs upon it.

One night in 2016 when we had all gone to bed, she suddenly appeared in my bedroom and plonked herself down on the carpet beside my bed. I was surprised but left her there. From that day onwards she slept on the floor in my bedroom. I tried to make life more comfortable for her by putting a soft dog basket beside the bed but she refused to use it. Basically she had given up the luxury of sleeping on a soft mattress so that she could sleep on the hard carpeted floor of her master. At last I felt that she had truly accepted me as her family and friend, although hardly a day went by without me having to tell her off.

Poppi and Sophie visit the Dordorgne and Les Vercors

In February 2015 I contacted several of my old friends from the College of St. Mark and St. John to invite them to my seventieth birthday bash which was being held at the Sutton Tennis and Squash Club in Devonshire Road, Sutton, at the end of the month. One of my friends was a fellow ex-Lancastrian, Bob Hughes, who had shared a flat with me at Sutton Green in 1970.

Apart from his house in Hertfordshire, Bob also informed me that he and his wife, Jane, also had a small farm in the Dordorgne that they visited several times a year. When he invited me to visit the place I tentatively accepted but said it would have to be at the end of the cricket season. In late July Bob repeated his offer and said that he and his wife would be staying there for the whole of September and October.

Thursday the 1st of October, therefore, saw Poppi, Sophie and myself board the 12.55 P&O ferry from Dover to Calais in my heavily-laden, top-of-the-range Hyundai i40. As there was no room at my customary stopping off point with Madame Fourdinier in Samer, I motored down the coast until I found an Ibis at Berck-sur-Mer. I fed the dogs and decided to give them a walk along the coast. That was a bad mistake!

As we passed close to the racecourse, Sophie jumped into a stagnant ditch and was covered in a foul smelling coating of black slime. There was only one thing for it, she had to be thoroughly washed and dried. With that intent in mind I smuggled the dirty dog back into the Ibis and stuck her in the small shower cubicle. Unfortunately the shower head was not one that could be held in the hand and passed over the body of the dog, as it was attached to the ceiling of the shower. I probably became as wet as the struggling Sophie as I attempted to hold her under the stream of water.

The following day we drove over 200 miles, and being a creature of habit, I ended up seeking lodging at the Chambre d'Hotes of Marie-Claire at Dissay-sous-Courcillon. It was about the fifth time that I had stayed there and on each occasion it was in a different building. The one that the dogs are lying in front of had become a Centre of Well Being. Needless to say I did not avail myself of the Neurocoaching which they advertised, nor of the Hammam Spa or of the Shiatsu Massage which were both available.

We left Dissay early the following morning and ploughed slowly southwards for another seven hours before we miraculously reached our destination at about 4 p.m., thanks to the marvellous Hyundai Satnav system. I say 'miraculous' as all that I keyed

into the Satnav were the words 'Barracat' (the name of the farm) and Dordorgne. I have recently tried to rediscover the farm using Google Earth and struggled. The photograph on the right shows the modest sign on a very quiet country road which indicated that we had reached our destination.

Beyond the five-barred gate there was a long dusty lane flanked by twenty Acer trees, which led up to the ancient farmhouse that Bob had fully restored and transformed into a beautiful modern home. Beyond that there were a couple of rather dilapidated barns that Bob seemed to be constantly working upon. Our home, for the five days

that we stayed there, was an old pig-stye which had been transformed into a quite tasteful, long narrow bedroom.

The photograph on the right shows Poppi in the bedroom with its rough stone walls which had been the inner walls of the pig-stye. The large white plastic bin on the left is one that I took with me on every holiday and contained all the dogs' food and necessities.

Bob had transformed himself from being a very well qualified geography teacher into a part time farmer and general labourer. Much of the time that we were there he spent renovating the barns but, as he had made the fatal mistake of throwing a few sticks for Poppi to chase on that first evening, she followed him everywhere and was continually dropping sticks at his feet.

The photograph on the right shows Bob working on a ladder, with Poppi lying on the ground looking up at him expectantly, with her paws resting on a rather large stick.

Sophie, on the other hand, tended to follow Bob's wife, Jane, around for a couple of reasons: firstly Sophie has always loved ladies, and secondly she probably associated Jane with the kitchen and food.

The photograph on the right shows Jane and Sophie in the large seventy tree orchard gathering walnuts to take back to England. By 2015, the orchard was the only productive part of the farm.

The dogs loved their short holiday in the Dordorgne. They were given almost total freedom to wander around the farm, although I must admit that I was a little worried about how safe the barns were, with their ancient rusty farm implements, plus I did not think that Sophie would fare at all well if she came across a rat.

I do not think that I ever saw Poppi look as contented and relaxed as she looked in the photograph on the right. She was lying at the base of the ladder looking upwards at Robert, just waiting for him to play with her again.

Sadly our holiday in the Dordorgne was over far too soon and we had to head towards the Alps and St. Andeol if we wanted to spend some time there before the arrival of the snow. It was great to have been able to spend some quality time with my old college friend and his wife.

Robert J. Hughes passed away in December 2023.

One of the joys of shunning motorways is that, although the journey is much slower, one is able to see so much more of the French countryside, and sometimes one is absolutely stunned by the view. This was the case when I drove through the outskirts of Le Puy En Velay along the winding second class road, the D589. Suddenly, as I rounded a bend, I was faced by the imposing iron statue of the Virgin Mary overlooking the town.

As there was probably 150 miles still to go, I decided to seek lodging for the dogs and myself near the local railway station in an Ibis which was built into the side of a hill. It was quite a novel experience to enter the building on the top of the slope and to take a lift down two floors to our room which was basically on the ground floor with windows overlooking the town.

This photograph shows the dogs having their evening meal in the Ibis, whilst I ate in the Railway Hotel next door. Poppi was eating from one of the silver metal bowls which I had bought for Benji and Gemma, whilst Sophie had a small plastic bowl which I had had to buy in France, and which she still uses today.

The following day we met up with Jolyon and Corinne in the chalet at St. Andeol and ate that evening at the home of their nearest neighbours Jacques and Monique Picot, who had prepared a meal of Pommes Dauphine especially for me.

The next two and a half weeks followed the pattern of the previous three visits to the chalet. On week days I tended to do household chores in the morning with visits to the supermarket in Monestier de Clermont, whilst in the afternoons we went walking. One of the most interesting places that we visited was La Fontaine Ardent.

After parking near the church of Saint-Barthelemy du Gua, we descended via a steep pathway to the stream at the bottom of the valley to see the fountain of fire. In the centre of a crudely built stone circle was a flame that was fed by methane gas escaping from a vent in the earth. As the dogs had a healthy respect for fire they observed it from a distance.

In the evenings after I had made a meal, tidied it away and built up a pile of logs for the fire, it was time to relax. After unsuccessfully trying to watch a little French television, I usually opted for watching episodes of 'The Office' or a western on my portable TV and DVD player, whilst having made sure that they had avoided passing in front of the fire, both dogs could usually be found on the quilt covered settee at the far side of the room. As Poppi was the senior partner in that relationship she usually got the cushion upon which to lay her head.

At 10 p.m. I would let the dogs out for their final toilet of the day before we all retired to the ice-box that was my bedroom, where I would sleep inside a sleeping bag, under a thick duvet. Quite often both dogs would sleep upon the bed which added slightly to the warmth of the situation.

At weekends Jolyon and Corinne would descend upon us, which made a pleasant break from our solitary existence. On Saturday mornings Jolyon would disappear on a five or ten kilometre run along some of the mountain trails, before returning to play boules

with me or to throw a ball or a stick for Poppi. The photograph on the right shows her running around with what was basically a ten foot long wooden spear, which she would throw at the nearest person.

Sophie, however, tended to remain in the chalet with Corinne, if she was preparing the food for the evening meal, as there was always a chance that she could be thrown a tit-bit. Her stomach tends to rule her behaviour, whilst Poppi probably loved play more than food.

After one final walk with Jolyon on Sunday morning October 25th, it was time to start our journey back to Blighty. Although our ferry was not booked until the 3rd of November, I was not confident that I would be able to stay another week and make it back in time to catch the boat. It was, therefore, with great regret that we bade farewell to Jolyon and Corinne. I wondered if we would ever see St. Andeol again. The result of the referendum in 2016 certainly made it more difficult.

The journey from St. Andeol to the Pas De Calais is probably 550 miles by the quickest route. As I have a great dislike of motorways, one can probably add another hundred miles on to that total, and so I was extremely pleased to make the return trip in under three days. The most nerve-racking part of the journey was the first twenty five miles as it was virtually impossible to avoid driving through Grenoble.

The first evening was spent in a pleasant Premier Classe Hotel, which I had stayed in before on the main road leading through Bourg En Bresse. The Monday evening, however, saw us staying in a less salubrious setting on an industrial estate in a F1 Hotel at Sens Nord. The following morning saw me driving North as far as Soissons to avoid having to travel through Paris. At Soissons I headed west towards the English Channel and, as I had nowhere else to stay, we ended back at the Ibis in Breck sur Mer.

As we still had about a week left before the ferry, and as the Ibis was costing me about 50 euros per night, I rang up Madame Fourdinier but found that she was fully booked. I then tried Madame Pruvost in Carly and found that she had a vacancy for the week. That was great as the room was very comfortable, the dogs were free and her breakfast was superb.

For late August the weather was brilliant that week. Most days I would drive into Montreuil-sur-Mer, park the car and then visit one of the many newsagents that stocked English newspapers and also spoke the language. I would then sit at a table outside Le Pot Du Clape with the dogs tethered to the table, reading the paper and partaking of a delicious bowl of vegetable soup with fresh French bread. The photograph on the left shows Sophie eyeing, with interest, a young family who were eating at a nearby table.

After that we would stroll around the battlements of the fortress at Montreuil, where General Haigh had his headquarters in World War One. The photograph on the right shows the dogs on top of the defensive ramparts with a steep drop just a couple of feet in front of them. Poppi was staring into the distance looking for an approaching enemy.

One day we drove into Le Touquet and had a stroll around the boulevards and shops, whilst on another afternoon we actually made it into Boulogne, which I had last visited in about 1955 on a day trip with my parents. Probably the strangest visit, however, was to the Welsh Fish and Chip Shop in Etaples. The meal did not quite reach the standards that one would expect at Harry Ramsdens but it was quite passable.

With a couple of days left before the trip home, and not really wanting to visit Calais twice, and with a little help from Madame Pruvost, we managed to find a vet named Didier Smal at Condette, near Boulogne, who was qualified to worm the dogs and to ascertain that they were fit enough to travel.

The photograph on the right shows my lonely looking Hyundai i40 waiting in Calais for the 11.35 to Dover at the end of a most enjoyable holiday in which I drove just over 2,000 miles.

Poppi is Diagnosed with Diabetes Mellitus

In September 2017 I became a little worried by the amount of water that Poppi was consuming. Fearing that it could be something serious I contacted Ejaz Hameed, the vet at the Wingrave Practice in Epsom. After a series of tests it was confirmed that she had developed diabetes mellitus but that she would be able to lead a relatively normal life if she was put on a course of caninsulin for life. The amount of caninsulin that she required was determined over the next six weeks by another series of expensive blood tests. Fortunately she was insured for £7,000 per condition. That sounds quite a lot but it is amazing how expensive diabetic treatment for dogs can be.

TIP NUMBER 34: If your dog begins to drink an excessive amount it could be a sign that it has Diabetes Mellitus.

I felt a little squeamish at the thought of having to stick a hypodermic needle into the scruff of Poppi's neck even once, but the thought of having to do it twice a day for the rest of her life was mind blowing; but after a while it became part of our strict daily routine. I must admit that I became quite adept at giving her an injection and quite often could not be bothered to muzzle her. She only gave me a warning nip on about two occasions. For the drug to be really effective it was important that she was given the injection every twelve hours just after her food, and that any change in her weight was to be reported to the vet, as it might mean that her dosage should be altered. Every morning, therefore, at about 7.30 a.m. just after their food, I would give her a biscuit, slip on her muzzle, grab the scruff of her neck, stick the needle in and give her 8 units of caninsulin. The same ritual occurred at 7.30 p.m. just after their evening meal, although this was not always possible if life intervened.

Sadly I was fully aware that blindness was often associated with diabetes. Lo and behold, at the end of 2017 it became obvious that Poppi's eyesight was failing dramatically as she kept bumping into items of furniture. By the middle of January 2018 Poppi was totally blind, although in a way it did not seem to faze her. Inside the house she obviously used her memory to move around with very little trouble.

I was amazed at Poppi's resilience to her problems. Every evening she would nose

around and find a very old, punctured, giant tennis ball, which she would place upon my lap. I would gently lob it into the air and, using her other senses, she would find it and proudly bring it back to me, wagging her tail. She knew where I was sitting because of the reading light by my side, and could obviously distinguish between light and darkness.

Occasionally when she brought it back she would not relinquish her grip upon the ball and a tug-of-war would ensue. She seemed so happy that it was difficult to realise that she was blind unless one looked at her eyes.

Poppi coped magnificently around the house and the garden, considering her disability. It was outside that the problems arose. I had to remember to keep her on a tight lead when walking down the Close as she tended to walk head first straight into any wheely bin or lamp post which was in her way. When she was on the lead it was my responsibility to guide her around any obstacle in her path. She seemed to have complete confidence in me, despite the fact that I occasionally failed in my task.

I was determined to keep her as physically and mentally active as possible, and she definitely wanted life to go on as normal. In the park Poppi still wanted to be let off the lead and, if I failed to do so, she would sit there stubbornly refusing to move. When she was free she would run about forty yards and crouch there waiting for me to throw a ball. I basically had to throw the ball at her if she was to have any chance of finding it, and then she virtually had to step on the ball to find it. If she did find it, I would have to continually whistle and shout, "Come here!" so that she could find me. Occasionally she would run up to other people and drop the ball at their feet.

To make life a little easier for her I bought a couple of balls with bells inside, which helped her to determine where the ball was going. The photograph on the right was taken from a video that I made of her in the park with one of the new balls. One can see her milky-white cataracts in each eye quite clearly.

Poppi visits Wimbledon Common

Shortly after Poppi went blind I contacted Ejaz Hameed, my favourite vet who also played cricket for me, and asked him if there was any treatment available to help Poppi regain her sight. He replied that there were a few Canine Hospitals around the country who successfully removed cataracts and replaced them with new lens but that it was very expensive. As Poppi was insured I asked him to go ahead and make an appointment with one of them to see whether she was a suitable candidate.

Ejaz was as good as his word and managed to obtain us an appointment at 12 o'clock on Tuesday 6th of February at a relatively local veterinary practice which lay close to Wimbledon Common. What made the appointment even more perfect was the fact that it was probably only about five miles away and was on the 93 bus route. As the nearest bus stop was only a short walk from Netley Close, there was no worry about driving there or finding a car park.

As we arrived there a little early, and as it was a fine day, we went for a short walk on the Common looking for Wombles before arriving at our destination. After a short wait we were invited into the consulting room by the vet who began by explaining what the procedure involved. Some eye drops were then put into a muzzled Poppi's eyes before we returned to the waiting room for about 15 minutes. After that we were invited back into the consulting room so that the vet could re-examine Poppi's eyes.

Poppi, after a minute or two of the examination, began to indicate that she was not happy, showed her teeth for a few seconds and then lunged forward snapping, as far as one can snap in a muzzle, at fresh air. On the whole, however, I felt that she was very restrained. The diagnosis of the vet was that, although Poppi was a suitable candidate for the procedure, she would not do the operation as Poppi was an aggressive dog. To support her decision she said that the notes forwarded to her from the Wingrave had indicated that Poppi must always be muzzled when being treated, plus the fact that I had already admitted that she did not like to be poked and prodded. The Vet also felt that if the operation were carried out then her aggressive behaviour could make all the necessary follow-up treatment very difficult to carry out, and could ruin the whole procedure.

I was very disappointed to hear this diagnosis. The Vet had basically said that she could do the operation but would not. For that diagnosis, a few eye drops and less than half an hour of her time I was charged £295.68, of which £234 was for the consultation. As the notes forwarded by the Wingrave had indicated that Poppi had an attitude problem, I was more than a little annoyed that they had even invited us for the consultation. At 12.44 I paid the bill and left with a feeling that I had been ripped off.

Poppi visits Hampshire

Ejaz was very disappointed when he heard about the decision of the vet in Wimbledon and promised that he would try again to find another practice which might accept her. Within a couple of weeks he came back with a possible facility which might possibly treat her at Havant in Hampshire. It was at least 60 miles further than Wimbledon but it was worth a shot. By this stage I was not over optimistic. Would Poppi's behaviour again scupper any hopes that I might have of getting her sight back?

On Monday March 20th, therefore, I packed both dogs into the car and set off quite early for a late morning appointment at the Optivet Referral Clinic in Havant. Basically I drove south down the A29 towards Bognor, turned right along the busy Winchester Bypass and then let the Satnav take over. The Clinic, which was on an industrial estate, was a very impressive looking single storied building which had a decent car park surrounded by a grassy verge where the dogs could relieve themselves.

Inside the front door there was a large comfortable waiting area beyond which lay a long, almost semi-oval reception hub, behind which sat two or three receptionists. As we approached the hub, Sophie rose on her hind legs and placed her paws upon the counter, wagging her tail furiously, and made eye contact with Faith, the pleasant young lady who greeted us. Poppi stood there impassively, not realizing her future was in the balance.

Around the perimeter of the building there were six consulting rooms, which included two ophthalmology examination rooms, plus two state of the art operating rooms and separate wards for cats and dogs. It was an exceedingly impressive and busy facility, with members of staff in scrubs constantly passing backwards and forwards to report to anxious dog and cat owners who were sitting in the waiting room.

After a short wait we were called into a consulting room by the imposing, be-smocked figure of one of the leading vets at the practice, Stamatina Giannikaki, who was an instant hit with Sophie. Stamatina quietly explained what the procedure entailed and then began to calmly and confidently perform a series of tests upon Poppi. Apart from the customary eyedrops and pieces of, what looked like, litmus paper placed under the eyelids, the eyes were scanned by bright lights and photographs were taken. Then a gun-like machine tested the pressure of each eye.

Poppi was her charming self and only showed her teeth and tried to snap about three times. I was on tenterhooks as I had told Stamatina what had happened at the other establishment. She felt that Poppi's behaviour would not be a problem but warned me that having the operation would mean an awful lot of extra work for me. She was certainly right about that, but in a way it strengthened the bond between Poppi and myself. It also stimulated my aging brain cells in the battle against senility.

As Poppi's operation was scheduled for early morning on Monday, March 26th, and as she was supposed to remain in the hospital until the following day, I asked Optivet whether they could recommend anywhere locally where we could stay. They came up with the fantastic building on the right, Hollybank House, a Georgian mansion which was set in ten acres of grounds at Emsworth, and which was approached up a long sweeping driveway. Inside the house was a mixture of comfort and elegance.

We travelled down to Emsworth on the Sunday afternoon with enough food for the dogs for a couple of days, and a mini-fridge which would keep Poppi's caninsulin at the required temperature both in the car and in the house. This tiny fridge was a great asset and accompanied us whenever we went away, and was particularly useful when we went on tour.

After we had settled into the luxurious bedroom and the dogs had been fed, we wandered out on to the large lawn so that the dogs could chase a ball with a bell within it, hopefully for the last time. This activity had to be abandoned after blind Poppi became entangled in one of the holly bushes which surrounded the lawn,

Although Poppi had to be starved the following morning, I was presented with an absolutely fabulous early breakfast by the master of the house, as we had to arrive at

Optivet before 8.00 a.m. so that Poppi could be prepped for the operation, which was to be conducted by the chief veterinarian surgeon, Rob Lowe. I was told that they would ring me with the result of the operation later in the day, and that I could pick her up on Tuesday morning.

As I had twenty four hours to kill I decided to visit an ex-colleague of mine from Glastonbury High School, Eric Champion and his wife Carol, who lived with Anya, a young St. Bernard, on a rather posh estate at Hedge End, near Southampton. In the evening I planned to walk Sophie down to the sea front at Emsworth and wander around the Harbour and the yacht basin.

After negotiating the early morning rush hour in Havant, I booked Poppi in for her treatment at Optivet and left a Tupperware container of her food, which she could eat when she came round from the operation. I gave her a little hug and departed towards Southampton.

When I arrived at Eric's house at about 10.30, Sophie and I were almost overpowered by the enormous, over-friendly St. Bernard who greeted us. Anya probably weighed about ten stone and was eight times the size of Sophie. As I had not seen Eric for two years, and had never seen his wife before, we had a great catchup session before deciding to take Anya and Sophie a walk around the surrounding fields.

As we completed the walk my mobile phone rang. It was one of the vets from Optivet who said that the good news was that the operation was a success; the bad news was that Poppi was not very happy and was not being very co-operative. They asked me to collect her as soon as possible and to return her the following morning.

My plans for the day were now scuppered. I had to apologize to Eric and Carol and beat a hasty retreat back to Havant, where I collected a very drowsy dog and her Tupperware container of food, plus some eye drops. I never did really find out why they decided that it was best for her to be returned to her owner as she was supposed to spend the night in the hospital. As a result Sophie and I spent the evening quietly in the bedroom at Hollybank House with Poppi, rather than walking around the harbour.

When I returned to the animal hospital the following day I really began to understand the enormity of the decision that I had made in having Poppi's cataracts removed, when I was presented with a bill for £3,950. As the blindness was considered by the insurance company as being a result of the diabetes, it made rather a large dent in the £7,000 which the insurance company allowed for that particular condition.

I was then given a list of the treatment which Poppi had to receive at home:

Pred Forte eye drops - give one drop 2x daily to both eyes
Voltarol eye drops - give one drop 6x daily to both eyes
Azopt - give one drop 2x daily to both eyes
Cephacare - give orally 1.5 tablet twice daily for 7 days, starting this evening
Loxicom - give dose ONCE daily for 2 weeks by mouth, starting tomorrow

This meant that apart from having to inject Poppi twice a day with caninsulin, she had to be given eyedrops TEN times a day, plus the extra medication. It was also usually necessary to leave a five to ten minute time gap between the different eyedrops which lengthened the time needed. It was a logistical nightmare which necessitated the use of daily spreadsheets with tick boxes.

Finally, we had to make the 130 mile round trip to Havant the following week for a follow-up consultation, and little did I know that we would have to undergo that journey about ten times that year for reviews and new prescriptions. Gradually the number of trips and eyedrops decreased until in about 2020 we only had to make the journey every six months, whilst Poppi merely had to have Voltarol and EDTA eye drops put in her eyes at meal times. They became part of the daily feeding regime.

The final instruction from the clinic was that *'Dogs should be given gentle exercise on a harness and kept relatively quiet for several days following surgery.'* To keep Poppi quiet after a couple of days was probably the most difficult task of all..

Despite the cost and the extra work I felt that it was totally worthwhile when, as we walked in the park a few days later, Poppi suddenly looked up to watch a squirrel running along a branch. Eventually when I could let her off the lead she seemed like her old, occasionally troublesome self, chasing a ball or better still, from her point of view, throwing a stick around.

Life Revolves around Poppi

In a way Poppi's illness really altered our relationship. For five or six years she had been the rather aloof other dog, who lagged behind Benji and Sophie in my affection. Now she had been thrust to the centre of the stage and we could not ignore each other. Our whole daily routine revolved around her medication, and I must admit that I began to love her, despite her independent character. I was completely confident that the aggressive façade was just a bluff.

For her part Poppi accepted the daily routine of me holding her snout whilst I forced her eye-lids open, without her trying to bite me. I really think that she appreciated what I was trying to do for her, or perhaps it was the fact that she received a small biscuit before and after every eye-drop. I was that confident in our relationship that I never muzzled her for eye-drops and not always for injections.

Our first real attempt to try to pursue a normal life was a visit to the Isle of Wight in July, on cricket tour. We stayed in the same tiny room at the Braemar in Shanklin, but now with a tiny red fridge, containing a phial of caninsulin, hypodermic needles, two or three bottles of eye drops and a Tupperware container of Royal Canin Sensitivity Control, on the bedside table.

There was a noticeable improvement in Poppi's attitude towards other dogs on this tour. She seemed more relaxed and confident. Every morning we went on the Big

Mead Rec. and there was no attempt to dominate Skye, the Alsatian, when they chased a ball. I doubt whether that had anything to do with the operation but more with the fact that she was, by then, over ten years old.

The photograph on the right shows the dogs inside the grounds of Carisbrooke Castle four months after the operation. Whilst Sophie is drinking from a water bowl Poppi is looking directly at the camera. If one looks very carefully at her eyes one can see that they look quite clear. The whiteness is merely the light reflecting off her eyes.

Letter to Medivet

In October 2018, as Poppi's insurance cover for her diabetes had been severely damaged by the eye operation, I wrote a rather critical letter to Medivet explaining that I had been a loyal customer of the Wingrave Practice for over thirty seven years and that I was appalled at the increase in the cost of some of the medicines that they provided. One of the medicines which I mentioned was the caninsulin which they had just increased in price to £53.18 for a small bottle which lasted less than a month. I accused them of profiteering at the expense of the poor pet owner by making an obscene amount of profit on a vital drug, which could be obtained online for £23.58. Somewhere in the organisation I must have found someone with a conscience as a special discount was applied to their caninsulin. Although it did not match the online price, one at least knew that the product was kosher.

I also complained that I had been charged just over £32 for a small bottle of Voltarol eye drops which was £10 more than that charged by Optivet, although to be fair as they were a specialist ophthalmic clinic they probably had a deal with the drug company. That was not the best price, however, as the local chemist charged £9.22 for the same product, however, one had to have a prescription.

For the cost of £16, however, Optivet provided me with a repeat prescription for two bottles of Voltarol, five times within six months. If one factored in the cost of the prescription I bought 10 bottles at £10.82 apiece.

TIP NUMBER 35: Check online prices and then try to negotiate a deal with your veterinarian practice. One would hope, however, that items purchased from your vet might be of a proven quality.

TIP NUMBER 36: Check whether the medication recommended by your vet for your dog is available from a Chemist. If so ask your vet for a prescription - preferably a repeat prescription. It could be worth it.

The Social Dynamics change after the Operation

The fact that I had to manhandle Poppi several times a day to either inject her or administer the eye-drops, was bound to alter our relationship. We definitely became much closer. Her behaviour certainly changed after the operation: she became more animated, less reserved and friendlier.

Every evening after the drugs were administered and the dogs had eaten their food, I would settle down to work on my laptop in front of the television. Whenever Poppi came into the room she would walk over to the side of my chair and nudge my elbow, which jerked my mouse, as though to say, "I'm here!" She would then pick up a battered old ball and try to drop it onto my laptop, as though to say, "Let's Play!" If that failed to get my attention she would stand in front of the television screen, stare at me and bark, which usually got some sort of reaction.

Sophie, who always used to be the centre of attention, would watch quietly from the sidelines. She did not seem to mind the extra attention that Poppi was getting, but she knew to avoid Poppi when she was in a frolicsome mood. As I spent more time working upon my books upon Worcester Park Athletic Club there was less opportunity for her to be a lap-collie.

Despite an occasional disagreement Poppi and Sophie were still the best of friends and spent a large part of every day, lying next to each other, behind my reclining chair, in their beds next to the window, overlooking Netley Close and the Park, where occasionally they would erupt into a frenzy of barking if they spotted a passing cat, dog or fox.

As an interesting aside, after every meal in the kitchen, Poppi would make a bee-line for those beds, throw herself onto her back and roll over, vigorously kicking her legs in the air, probably to help her digestion or perhaps even to clean her whiskers.

When Poppi had been blind and we had played with a ball with a bell inside it, Sophie had seemed to realise the problem and occasionally backed off to let Poppi find the ball. Now her sight had been restored no quarter was given, although I tended to favour Poppi by aiming the ball at her, as she lay crouched about forty yards away. Sophie made it a little more difficult for herself to get the ball by jumping up excitedly on her hind legs whilst she waited for the ball to be thrown. As soon as the ball was thrown, however, she shot off like a whippet, but usually to no avail. When Poppi gathered the ball she would run towards me wagging her tail and would drop the ball about ten yards away, thus allowing Sophie to complete the retrieve.

Whenever we walked through the woods where it would not have been very sensible to throw the ball, Sophie would walk backwards on her hind legs trying to encourage me to throw it, whilst Poppi disappeared into the bushes, looking for sticks. The photograph on the right shows Sophie appealing for the ball to be thrown.

Christmas Day and the Dogs

Every Christmas Day the dogs and myself always drove down to Wallis Wood to spend the day with my half cousin, Juliet, and her family on her small farm. When Benji and Gemma were alive they were always welcome to enjoy the celebrations, but I was always reticent about allowing Poppi into her home in case she attacked Tiny, Juliet's aged terrier. Poppi, therefore, usually spent the whole of the day ensconced upon the rear seat of the car, which was actually her favourite place, whilst Sophie was being fussed over by all the guests.

In 2018, as per usual, I left Poppi in the car, but late in the evening I was encouraged to take her inside. She seemed quite pleased and wandered around the long, narrow room exploring her environment and making friends with everyone she met, whilst Tiny was safely placed upon someone's lap. After a while she became bored and, as she could not find a ball or stick to play with, she decided that a small plastic dustpan made a great toy to throw around, much to everyone's amusement. I have a very dark, short video of the incident which shows Felix, Juliet's son, sliding the dust pan back to her with his foot along the wooden floor and an excited Poppi flinging it back at him to the resounding sound of laughter.

After displaying that she could be trusted to behave in polite society, Poppi no longer had to stay in the car but became a regular star guest at Juliet's Christmas party. The photograph on the right shows Poppi and Sophie, wearing their Xmas bibs, waiting with great anticipation for the festivities to begin in 2019.

Poppi, Sophie and Covid

Little did we know at the time of the Christmas party in 2019 that it would be our last real chance to socialise for quite a long time. The pandemic had already started in Wuhan province in November 2019, and by February 2020 was sweeping through Europe whilst our government sat upon their hands.

On my birthday on February 28th, I was taken for a meal by an ex-colleague, Karen Powell, one of my oldest friends, who informed me that she had just come back from the Caribbean where her plane had been met by masked medics who tested everyone's temperature. Back in Blighty, however, people were free to enter the U.K. from all parts of the globe without hindrance.

It was at this point that I decided that I should isolate myself, but unfortunately it was too late, as I had already been contaminated upon my final shopping trip in Sainsburys, either by the gentleman who seemed to be coughing his guts up near the in-house pharmacy, or by the delightful young lady at the self service hub who turned in my direction and coughed, without any attempt to place her hand over her mouth.

At its peak my first encounter with Covid was not particularly pleasant as I found it very difficult to breathe. I dosed myself with Lemsip and used a Vick inhalant infusion to try to ease my breathing, and tried not to panic. My main worry was what might happen to Poppi if I failed to survive. The last thing that I did that night was to print out all the instructions about how to feed the dogs and Poppi's medication regime. The following instructions were then left upon the work-surface in the kitchen, in case I failed to last the night.

Poppi and Sophie's Food and Treatment

Food twice a day at approx. 7.30.

Three quarters of a scoop **between** them for each meal.

The food is in the large white container. It is a mixture of Happy Dog and Burns (Chicken and Rice)

Add half a tin of Royal Canin Sensitivity Control **between** them.

To Poppi's food add 2 tablets of YouMove. On worksurface.

Medicine

Put muzzle on Poppi. Give her a little biscuit and then put one Volterol Eye drop in each eye. Medicine in plastic container in fridge.

After food replace muzzle and put 8 units of Caninsulin in a syringe.

After a gap of ten minutes from putting the first eye drops in, put the other eye drops in. They are EDTA

There are replacements in the fridge for all these items.

Really she should have the EDTA in three times a day, but twice will do.

It was with great relief that I awoke the following morning to see that I was still in the land of the living and was breathing a little easier. My main problem, as I was isolating, was how to obtain food. Fortunately Ryan Ford, one of my team who lived locally, managed to do a couple of small shops for me and left them in the porch, whilst I went through the tortuous hurdle of managing to set up regular online deliveries from Sainsburys.

By the time of the First Lockdown on March 23rd, I had already been in voluntary isolation for about three weeks. Unlike most people, however, I quite enjoyed the opportunity the Lockdowns afforded me to spend more time bonding with my dogs. It also allowed me to finish my first book on the sporting organisations which existed locally before W.P.A.C. came into existence in 1921. I was determined to get it finished in time for the club's centenary in the forlorn hope that it might be of interest to the members. I should have known better!

The first Lockdown did alter our daily routine considerably, however, as in order to avoid the increased number of people exercising in the park, it was necessary to take

the dogs a walk as soon as it became day-light. In the summer we could often be found walking in Nonsuch Park as early as about 4.30 a.m. Even at that time in the morning it was surprising how many people one bumped into, which increased my paranoia. The photograph on the right shows the dogs, early one morning in the park, with Sophie waiting for Poppi to relinquish her hold on the ball.

Although playing golf was banned until May 13th in 2020, it did not stop me from spending hours in the garden trying to chip air-flow balls into the conservatory helped, of course, by Poppi who enthusiastically retrieved every ball. She would gather up the ball, run back two or three paces towards me and then flick the ball with impressive force towards me. Her accuracy, however, left a little to be desired.

As all cricket matches were banned until mid-July I did try, unsuccessfully to improve my hand/eye co-ordination by using a catching frame. It was yet another opportunity to bond with Poppi who proved that both her eye sight and her reflexes were far superior to mine. It was strange to think that she had been totally blind less than a year before.

Although certain restrictions concerning social distancing were put in place at the golf club when play resumed in May that year, they did not really affect me as for most of the year Poppi, Sophie and occasionally John Murtagh were my only companions.

Although the 2020 cricket season was severely curtailed, my Sunday Social XI did manage to play eleven matches that year. Unfortunately as five of those matches were at home where dogs were not allowed, and as the weather was rather hot on three or four other occasions, Poppi and Sophie had to remain at home listening to Radio Two. They did, however, attend the final two matches where they saw the Park players put in a couple of stunning performances against Forest Green and Oakwood Hill.

For the second and third Lockdowns I abandoned the early walks in the park, as I had discovered that although one was not allowed to play golf, it was permissible to walk on the golf course for ones daily exercise. Therefore, Poppi, Sophie and myself spent about an hour every day wandering around 166 acres of some of the finest countryside in Surrey at Cuddington Golf Club.

In the photograph on the right, which could easily grace a Christmas card, Poppi and Sophie were lying on the snow covered first tee on a bright sunny January day in 2021, during the third national lockdown. We hardly saw anyone on our walk around the course but there were plenty of tracks which indicated the presence of foxes, badgers and deer, plus some Fieldfares in the bushes which were winter visitors.

Insurance Premium not Renewed

It was in the final lockdown that I received notification from the insurance company that Poppi's premium from 8th February 2021 to the 7th February 2022 would be £1,495.68, and that there would be an excess of £99 upon any new condition. As I could no longer claim any bills relating to her diabetes, I decided to gamble and did not insure her.

The Final Visit to the Isle of Wight 2021

After the restrictions of the previous eighteen months which had been imposed upon holiday making, it was a relief to visit the Isle of Wight on a cricket tour yet again in late May 2021, although I had no intention of playing cricket. I had, however, taken my golf clubs on tour as I intended to play at Freshwater Bay on the Wednesday, as I had discovered that dogs were allowed at that golf club. (See Page 132 for a short account of the day out at Freshwater Bay)

Apart from watching the lads play at Ventnor on the Monday, we visited most of our old haunts such as Carisbrooke Castle, Appuldurcombe House and the Needles. The photograph on the right shows Poppi and Sophie lying on the chalky ground near the Tennyson Monument before we walked on a quite windy day to the Needles and back again, which was quite a feat for a thirteen year old dog and her owner.

I must admit that I was becoming slightly worried about the general state of Poppi's health at this stage. She had lost a little weight, which meant that her daily dosage of caninsulin had to be adjusted, and her eyes had begun to cloud over again. I think the photograph on the right is a good indication of how much her eyes had deteriorated. This is a photograph of Poppi following a complete stranger as we began our descent from the Tennyson Memorial. She was at least fifty yards away from Sophie and myself, but at least she came running towards us when I whistled.

Chick, Chick, Chick, Chick, Chicken

In the autumn of 2021, it was obvious that Poppi was gradually losing weight. She had been on a mixture of Royal Canin Sensitivity Control meat, Burns Chicken and Rice biscuits, plus the secret ingredient Ostrich - actually Happy Dog Africa which contains ostrich, and is hypoallogenic.

The Happy Dog Africa biscuits, which looked like dark brown buttons, were also perfect treats to give her before, and after, every injection or eye drop.

Quite often the only way I could entice her to eat her meals was to mix some bits of chicken into her food. For over a year, therefore, I would buy ready cooked chicken breast pieces from Sainsburys, rip them up into smaller pieces and hide them in her food. (In a way she ate better than I did.) I would then call out "Chick, Chick, Chick, Chick, Chicken" to entice her into the kitchen.

She ate very slowly and methodically, quite often dropping biscuits or meat onto the floor, which delighted Sophie who was fully aware that Poppi's dish was out of bounds, but that any crumbs on the floor were fair game. Usually I would add even more chicken to the plate if I felt that Poppi had not eaten a satisfactory amount. It quite often made feeding her a rather long, drawn-out process, but it curtailed her weight loss. Once Poppi had finished feeding, Sophie was then given permission to lick the bowl clean.

Poppi becomes Soppy

The photograph on the right was taken in late December 2021. Poppi was no longer the feisty, independent character of her youth with an aggressive reputation: she had mellowed. She was old, tired, extremely scruffy as she refused to be brushed, and just wanted to be loved.

Although she occasionally tried to entice me to play ball with her in the evenings, whilst I sat in front of the television, more often than not she just walked up to me and placed her head upon my knee, looked at me with her one good eye and asked me to stroke her. Her left eye just seemed to be a grey sightless orb.

Poppi and the Plastic Plant Pot Holders

At the bottom of the garden beyond the leylandii trees there was a small framework of shelves where I stored the hanging baskets in the winter. Some of the baskets were made of iron with metal chains, but some were lightweight white plastic bowls from which white plastic strings stretched upwards towards a white plastic hook. They were basically cheap and nasty, but Poppi loved them. Whenever my back was turned she would grab one by the hook and shake it about vigorously.

One evening in February 2022, I was watching television in the lounge at about 10.30 when Sophie began to growl. She had obviously heard something. I turned the sound on the television down and heard some banging downstairs. Fearing that I had left the front door unlocked and we were being burgled, I bravely went to the top of the stairs, switched on the light and was amazed at what confronted me. There, half way up the stairs and struggling to move was Poppi with her head stuck inside the cords of one of the white plastic plant pot holders. I did what anyone would do in that situation, I took a photograph of the poor victim before releasing her from her predicament.

What was really amazing about that photograph was the fact that Poppi had managed to negotiate the dog flap, the conservatory, the downstairs bedroom, the corridor and the stairs with the plastic pot holder hindering her ability to walk.

The following morning, which was extremely cold and frosty, Poppi was not quite as lucky as she had managed to trap a leg inside the plastic strings, as well as her head, which made it impossible for her to negotiate the dog-flap. I am not sure how long she had been lying there in the freezing conditions, but she did not appear to have suffered any permanent damage. After those two incidents all the white plastic pot holders were transferred to a top shelf where they were safely out of her reach.

Poppi—a Dogged Dog

According to the Oxford English Dictionary the word *'dogged'* means *'having or showing tenacity and grim persistence'*. In a way Poppi's doggedness was one of her most annoying yet admirable qualities. If she set her mind upon achieving a target she would ignore any setbacks in trying to achieve her goal.

This characteristic was apparent from Poppi's first few days in Cheam when she was determined to dominate Benji. The fact that he threw her to the ground and pinned her there with his teeth around her throat a couple of times was apparently a minor setback, as she continued trying to dominate him, until he decided that it was pointless trying to resist. All Benji wanted was a quiet life.

This doggedness of character was no more apparent than in the final year of her life, by which stage she was a relatively frail old dog, whose weight had plummeted from 16.5 Kgs to 13.5 Kgs. The fact that she had managed to get from the garden to the first floor of the house with a plant pot holder draped around her head and shoulders was an impressive display of her determination to achieve her goal.

Shortly after the plant pot holder incident she stumbled when approaching the top of the stairs and fell head over heels backwards down ten steps, like a large rag doll to the bottom of the stairs. I was horrified and was sure that she must have broken something. To my surprise she climbed to her feet, shook herself and slowly climbed to the top of the stairs as though nothing had happened. After that accident, however, I did notice that she tended to use the wall as a support when climbing or descending the stairs, as in the photograph on the right. It obviously helped her balance but did nothing for the cleanliness of the paintwork.

In the final few months of her life Poppi became relatively unsteady upon her feet. This was probably most noticeable in the kitchen when she was trying to eat her food, and she would sway slightly from side to side and stagger occasionally. In the park, however, she still wanted to chase a ball and would refuse to move until I let her off the lead. She was not too bad at running in a straight line, but if she had to turn to gather up the ball, there was quite a good chance that she would fall over.

I tried to make life as easy as possible for Poppi by aiming the ball close to her. When she ran towards me it was sometimes easy to forget that she was on her last legs, as she would prance around with her tail in the air and her head held high. Although it was obvious that she still loved retrieving the ball, I tended to restrict her freedom off the lead to about two minutes as I was worried that she might injure herself. She seemed quite happy then to walk by my side whilst her step daughter Sophie continued to chase the ball.

Despite the fact that Poppi struggled to chase a ball in the park without stumbling or falling over, she seemed to manage to walk around nine holes at Cuddington with consummate ease, although her behaviour left much to be desired, as she would still jerk forward on the lead, as she always had done, whenever my playing partner or I took a shot. In a way it was surprising that she knew when a shot was being played as her eye-sight was extremely poor. Perhaps her senses picked up other signals such as the silence before a shot was played.

Another of her annoying habits was to bark excitedly if ever I deemed to play another ball from the same spot, or if I wandered too far away from the trolley. The photograph on the left was taken after I had played two shots from the same place and walked off to pick up one of the balls, which led to a barking fit from my fourteen year old dog, who was pacing backwards and forwards on her lead.

As her behaviour could be rather distracting to other players, I usually found it less stressful to play by myself most of the time. My oldest partner, John Joseph Murtagh, was definitely not a dog lover. Whenever we played together I had to try to position my trolley and the dogs as far away from him as possible in order that any sudden lurch by Poppi could not be blamed for a slice or a hook.

My favourite opponents were two former team mates from Worcester Park C.C., Steve Lethaby and Colin Clark, neither of whom seemed at all fazed by Poppi's behaviour. The photograph on the following page shows Colin with Poppi and Sophie at Banstead Golf Club on a warm day in July 2022. Although I had been worried about Poppi's ability to cope with the heat and the distance, we managed to play eighteen holes that day. It was just another example of Poppi's determined and dogged character: she would have walked until she dropped.

That photograph, which was taken on the final hole of the round, shows Poppi looking in better condition than the camera-shy Sophie. It is interesting to note that Poppi in nearly every photograph had her ears erect and was looking directly in my direction. She was a true Border Collie waiting for her master's next command.

As a distraction technique to try to kerb Poppi's lunging forward whenever my partner took a shot, I would grab a small tuft of dead hair on her hind quarters and swiftly pull it out. This, of course, led to her trying to bite me, but by this stage she was too old and slow to catch me. Although it sounds cruel, I adopted that technique whenever we were outside and Poppi was moulting, which appeared to be all the time, as she steadfastly refused to allow me to brush her. She was a remarkably scruffy dog with dead, grey tufts of hair dotted throughout her coat, particularly around her hind quarters. When her hair became too matted I would muzzle her and gently try to remove some of the clumps of hair with scissors, until she became too agitated.

The photograph on the right shows Poppi and Sophie on the first tee at Cuddington Golf Club in August 2022 in front of the magnificent clubhouse. That was a rather nerve racking place to tee off from when Poppi was with me, as apart from playing in front of a crowded terrace, the tee was very close to the eighteenth green, where Poppi's occasional excited yelps might not have been appreciated by any members who happened to be putting on that green.

Although Poppi and Sophie attended several away cricket matches in 2022, the only photograph that I have of them is the rather boring one on the left hand side, which shows them on the paving slabs in front of the pavilion at Mynthurst in early September. I had tethered them there, rather than on the grass, as Poppi had been criticised on more than one occasion for digging holes in the ground. The photograph, however, does show the rather unkempt and dishevelled state of Poppi's coat.

Although the dogs do not even feature in this photograph of the victorious Sunday Social team at Forest Green on September 18th, it does include some of my oldest summer friends, as at least half of the team have been with me over twelve years, whilst John and Larry have been team mates since the last century, and Michael, who is now a successful businessman, has played for me since 2004.

Back Row: D. Stemp, Pradeep Khatri, Haider Aamir, Michael Sachdeva, John Rivenell, Ganapati Bhat
Front Row: Ashik Wani, Iqbal Jan, Larry Streeting

On the whole Poppi and Sophie tended to receive more attention from opposing players than from the Worcester Park team who were used to seeing them at matches. One or two of the players such as Haider and J.R, who were animal lovers, occasionally made a fuss of them or offered to take them a walk around the boundary, but some of the others, however, who probably lacked a dog in their childhood, were scared of dogs: and, therefore, of Poppi and Sophie.

Earlier that season, when we played away at Cobham Avorians an interesting situation arose when I discovered that Ashik was one of those unfortunate people who suffered from cynophobia. Whilst I had taken my dogs to the game, Ashik had brought his two young children, Mehreen (aged 8) and Rayyan (aged 10). Although Rayyan was rather tentative about even stroking Sophie, Mehreen had become accustomed to dogs at a friend's house, and as a result made a fuss of both dogs and wanted to take them a walk.

As I was a little worried how Poppi might react if I left her in the charge of a couple of youngsters, I decided to go for a walk with them. Mehreen took Poppi, who was as good as gold, and Rayyan, who was still a little tentative, took Sophie. After twenty minutes it was obvious that Rayyan's confidence had soared and he volunteered to take Poppi. Poor Ashik! When we returned he was subjected to numerous pleads from both of his children to get a dog.

Another of the team who was definitely not a dog lover was Pradeep, who had suffered a horrible canine experience the previous season, when he asked me for a lift to an away game. I never liked taking players to matches as, apart from all the spare equipment that I needed as the captain, I also had the two dogs. Poppi always slept stretched out on the rear seat, and Sophie always sat on the front passenger seat even if someone deigned to sit there.

Pradeep's large kit bag lessened the amount of space available for the dogs. I honestly did try to keep both dogs on the back seat, but we had been driving less than a couple of minutes before Sophie had forced her way onto Pradeep's lap and sat there for another forty five minutes, as I suspected that she might. Initially she tried to lick him but he kept backing away. I must admit that I found the situation mildly amusing whilst Pradeep accepted his fate stoically. He never did ask me for a lift again though.

An Important Decision

Ever since Poppi had been diagnosed with diabetes in October 2017 until the summer of 2021 I had managed to keep her weight relatively constant between 15.5 and 16.5 kilograms. Over the next year, however, she lost two more kilograms, and I began to be quite concerned by her weight loss. In early September 2022, therefore, I took her to see Ejaz and was informed that part of the problem could have been due to tooth decay. Ejaz recommended that Poppi should have at least two teeth removed and the remainder of them scaled and polished. The estimated cost of the operation, not including extractions and medication, was £398..65.

The cost of the operation did not really worry me as I had saved about £1,500 by not renewing her insurance policy. What really worried me was the thought that she might not survive the operation. In the end I agreed that she should have the operation. It was, therefore, with great trepidation that I delivered her into Ejaz's hands at about 8 a.m. on Friday September 16th. At about lunchtime, thinking that I would never see her again, I received the good news that she had survived the operation, and that I could collect her that evening.

When I collected a rather drowsy dog later that day, I was given a post-op dental information sheet plus the rather startling information that they had removed ten of Poppi's teeth. Only two had been extracted, the other eight had fallen out in the cleaning process, all for £720. I was presented with a small phial which contained her teeth and which I photographed later that evening in Sophie's tiny French plastic bowl.

I did not begrudge the money if it made Poppi's final few days easier, but one could not help but wonder whether the trauma of undergoing such an operation perhaps hastened her death thirty three days later.

Poppi's Final Days

Poppi recovered remarkably well following her dental treatment. For the first few days after the operation I fed her primarily on soft food, such as Royal Canin Sensitivity Control meat and scrambled eggs. After a week or so, I replaced the scrambled eggs with Burns Chicken and Rice kibble and Happy Dog Africa plus plenty of tiny pieces of chicken. Although there was no noticeable increase in her weight, at least the weight loss seemed to have stabilised.

Although Poppi looked to be very frail and unstable, she still managed to cope with the stairs at least half a dozen times each day, usually with me walking closely behind her. After she had been escorted into the garden to go to the toilet at the end of the day, she refused to stay downstairs but insisted on climbing two flights of stairs in order that she could sleep on my floor.

She was still the same determined, independent, unpredictable and frequently annoying character that she had always been. The photograph on the left, which was taken four days after the dental treatment, shows her barking at someone who was getting out of a car about twenty yards away. In a way it was surprising that she could see them. The photograph on the right shows her challenging me to shut her up.

In both photographs her rear legs are braced widely apart to help her balance and her coat looks extremely unkempt.

A couple of incidents which occurred in the last week of her life remain etched in my memory. On one occasion I went into the kitchen and found Poppi sitting there quite contentedly, with a cupboard door wide open, chewing a dentastick. Although I pretended to tell her off, I could not help but admire her opportunism and skill at being able to steal those treats.

On the second occasion I left both dogs at home whilst I went to play golf early one morning, and was away from home for about two hours.. When I arrived back at the house, I was gobsmacked to see Poppi sitting casually in front of the garage awaiting my return. Due to senility on my part I had left the side gate open, and Poppi had taken full advantage of the situation.

Poppi had always had a penchant for exploring the neighbourhood if ever she had the chance, and no amount of my calling or whistling would make her come home. She was blatantly disobedient and deep down I loved her for it. I had always to seek her out and grab her by the harness and almost drag her home. On this occasion, however, she had obviously explored to her heart's content, become bored and returned home to await my return. She had been spotted not only rummaging around behind the flats next door, but had wandered down to the end of the Close to pay a social call on Nuala and Belle, whose owners Liz and Sean regularly left food out for the foxes.

Poppi's Sad Fate

On Monday 17th October Poppi seemed slightly more unsteady on her feet and more reluctant to eat than usual. As I already had an appointment booked with Ejaz, however, for the following day, I did not ring the Vets for another appointment. It was a decision that I came to regret.

We managed a short walk of about a quarter of a mile in the park that afternoon before Poppi ground to a halt and I had to nurse her gently and very slowly back to the house, supporting her by her harness. She still managed to climb the stairs, however, when we returned home and lay behind my chair all evening until eleven o'clock, when I decided to let the dogs into the garden for their final toilet of the day.

Holding Poppi's harness I helped her down the stairs, along the corridor, through the bedroom into the conservatory, which had been brightly lit up by Sophie triggering the security light when she exited the dog flap. I opened the door for Poppi, as it was obvious that she would not be able to manage the dog flap, and she immediately collapsed in a heap on the artificial grass.

It was difficult to know what to do. Poppi had not weed and I could not just leave there on the lawn. With the aid of her harness I managed to get her back inside the conservatory, where she lay panting heavily. She was obviously distressed. I stroked her for about half an hour whilst I decided what to do. In the end I switched on the dimmer lights inside the conservatory, and left Poppi and Sophie there whilst I prepared a bed in the downstairs' bedroom, in order that I could stay close to her.

At about 3 a.m. I looked through the window and was relieved to see that Poppi had moved, and appeared to be sleeping peacefully in the position that she usually adopted on my bedroom floor, flat on her side with her legs stretched out. I decided not to disturb her and went back to bed for another three hours.

When I looked through the window at 6 a.m. and saw Poppi lying in exactly the same position my heart sank, as I realised that she was dead. When I felt her body it was obvious that she had been dead for several hours, and by the look on her face it seemed as though she must have been in some pain when she died as her eyes were open and her tongue was hanging from her mouth. I desperately wished that I had contacted an emergency vet and had her put to sleep. She had become my favourite dog and had not deserved to suffer.

Apart from cancelling her appointment with Ejaz, one of the first things that I did, and with great relish, was to give her a stiff brushing, in the knowledge that she would no longer try to bite me. In a strange way it made me feel better. I still wanted to care for her. It was something that I had never been able to do in the ten years that she had lived with me. She might be dead but that was no excuse for her to look scruffy.

As Poppi's body was already entering the rigour mortis stage, I closed her eyes and tried to re-insert her tongue into her mouth, before covering her body with a sheet and left her in exactly the same position as I had found her, before making arrangements with Juliet to bury her close to Benji that Saturday morning.

Even after she had died Poppi still managed to cause trouble. According to most websites rigour mortis in dogs was supposed to last for between 36 and 72 hours. Not with Poppi, however, as she was still quite stiff four days later. I had to gently try to manoeuvre her legs closer to her body without fracturing any of her limbs. I did manage to move them slightly and placed her in the boot of the car wrapped in a blanket with a few of her favourite toys which included a ball with a bell inside it.

When Sophie and I arrived at Juliet's farm that Saturday morning we found that Juliet's son, Felix, had already been hard at work and had produced quite an impressive rectangular hole in which to bury Poppi. It was quite a feat digging a hole that size in the Wealden Clay and had taken several hours.

Sophie and I said our final farewell to our marvellous friend, wrapped her in a sheet and placed her gently with some of her toys in the hole that Felix had dug.

After we had filled in the hole we placed a few rocks around it to mark the site of the grave, upon which I placed a few flowers a couple of days later.

It is a really beautiful place where Poppi is buried and I like to think that as the sun goes down her spirit, along with those of Benji and Gemma emerge from their graves to run around the field chasing imaginary balls and rabbits. Or they could go a couple of miles down the road to meet up with Ben, my first Border Collie.

Poppi presented me with one more problem. Although she had been dead for four days, the blanket in which I had wrapped her in the boot of the car had become stained with blood, as was the matting beneath the blanket.

When I mentioned that to Ejaz, he said that it might have been blood in her urine which had leaked from her. I just thought that it was Poppi being awkward as usual, and that she wanted to leave me one more memory of her.

I think that it is fair to say that I have been more affected by the death of my dogs than by any member of my family. It is difficult, however, to explain how I felt about the loss of Poppi. After a rocky start I had grown to love her as much, if not more than my previous three Border Collies, who were basically lovely, obedient and loyal dogs. Unlike Ben, Benji or Gemma, however, she had a streak of independence that I admired, although it quite often manifested itself in annoying and occasionally manic behaviour. I was not the only one affected by her death though, as Sophie seemed to become very depressed and insecure.

Changes in Sophie's Behaviour

In the last eighteen months I have noticed three or four changes in Sophie's behaviour which may, or may not, have been triggered by Poppi's death. The first, and most noticeable change that occurred was the fact that she kept very close tabs upon my whereabouts, and often followed me from room to room. If ever I left the living room and walked downstairs I knew that she would be watching me from the top of the stairs, and would give a worried bark if I went into the porch.

In the mornings, however, while I tended to work upon my laptop and sit with my feet upon my Revitive for an hour, á la Ian Botham, Sophie would usually retire to the conservatory where, from the comfort of her favourite chair, she could watch the front door. If I decided to go on an errand, therefore, as soon as I had closed the front door, she would run upstairs to the window overlooking the drive and start to bark, which usually led me re-opening the door to ask her to be quiet, and to tell her that I was only going to the shop. That usually had the desired effect, although she would stay looking out of the window until I returned.

Sophie appeared to be most subdued and depressed in the evenings, when she would lie listlessly either on her settee or on her bed behind my chair for hours on end, whilst I worked on my computer or watched television. The only times that she stirred was if I went into the kitchen, where she would follow me in the hope that a morsel of food might come her way. She might have been sad but she was always hungry!

The photograph on the right shows a lacklustre looking Sophie lying on the doggy blankets which covered the settee, a month after the death of her friend, which seemed to have exacerbated the number of grey hairs around her eyes.

For six or seven years Poppi had slept on the floor of my bedroom, whilst Sophie was supposed to sleep in the living room, either in the cage or on the settee, or in her bed next to the window. I say 'supposed to' because she would occasionally sleep in the spare bedroom or in the conservatory. If ever I got up in the night I would hear the patter of tiny paws and by the time I switched the light on in the living room she would be lying on the settee, pretending that she had been there all night. In her mind she must have thought that it was naughty not to sleep in the living room. She tries so hard to be good!

One morning about six weeks after Poppi's death, Sophie climbed onto my bed at about 5 a.m. I presumed that she had wanted me to get up. The following morning she arrived a little earlier, and the morning after that etc, until eventually she went to bed at the same time as I did, although she would always look at me until I gave her permission to jump onto the bed. She sleeps in the same spot every night with her head resting on a towel covered pillow. The main downside with this arrangement is that I have to brush where she has slept every day with a special brush that gathers up dog hairs.

Another change which surprised me was the fact that Sophie started to scratch the artificial grass with her hind paws after she had weed. She had never indulged in that behaviour before. It was obviously an attempt to mark her territory. To tell the truth her first few attempts to scratch the ground looked very awkward. She does not do it very often but has improved her co-ordination. Could it be that she felt that ownership of the garden had reverted to her following Poppi's death, or was she just trying to leave a message for Sonny, the fox, who was prone to pass through the garden in the early hours of the morning and regularly stole my golf balls.

Another strange change in her behaviour which might have been connected to Poppi's death was the fact that she would no longer eat carrots. In the past whenever I was cooking, both dogs would appear whenever I started to peel carrots and I would throw each of them a small piece. Following Poppi's death, however, Sophie would catch the piece of carrot and then spit it out. Perhaps she had never really liked carrots but only ate them because Poppi did.

Sophie on the Golf Course

Sophie and I spent hundreds of hours in the twelve months following Poppi's death either playing by ourselves at Cuddington, or trudging around various golf courses such as Guildford, Banstead and Gatton Manor mainly with Colin Clarke or the Worcester Park C.C. Golf Society. My end of year report at Cuddington, however, revealed that although there were no golfing highlights I had at least made 133 bookings.

Most of those bookings tended to be for nine holes in the afternoon, in all sorts of weather, accompanied only by Sophie. The photograph on the right shows Sophie watching me as I was trying to play on the course in early January 2023. I aborted the attempt on the first hole, but at least Sophie had a short walk in her bright red coat, that she rarely wore as she has never seemed to suffer from the cold.

Quite often I did not really want to play, but every day after we had eaten lunch, Sophie would put pressure upon me to change for golf by standing in front of me and wagging her tail with an expectant air. As soon as I went upstairs to change into my golf trousers she would run up and down the stairs repeatedly in an excited manner. Just the sight of my golfing trousers or the action of putting on my Garmin watch was enough to inform her that we were about to play golf.

For Sophie a great game of golf involved meeting as many people as possible on the golf course, but quite often she was disappointed and only had me for company. She instantly recognised certain members, such as Dave Goodall, Michael Grigg and Leslie Pratt, with whom we had played in the past, and knew that all she had to do was to look them in the eye and wag her tail to ensure that she would be petted, whilst James Crossett, a trainee PGA professional, also went out of his way to give her a cuddle whenever he spotted her. Sophie also had many friends amongst the ladies, and was always made a fuss of especially by Joan Swann and Chloe Rigby, the Operations Assistant at the club, who is also a fellow Border Collie owner.

I must admit that Sophie still jerks forward whenever I take a shot on the golf course, but she is nowhere near as distracting as Poppi had been. For most of the time, however, she tends to look extremely sad and depressed without her friend. The photograph on the right shows a miserable looking Sophie tethered to my trolley on the seventeenth tee at Cuddington on Christmas Eve, 2022, less than ten weeks after we had lost Poppi.

Occasionally I would try to cheer her up, if we were at the far reaches of the course, and if there was no-one in sight, by letting her off the lead and throwing or kicking a ball for her to chase. Suddenly she would become alive and interested. The photograph on the left, which was taken that first Christmas without Poppi, shows her watching a ball intently in the hope that I was going to kick it for her to chase.

Nearly always on the final green after I had finished putting, I would reward her by putting the ball in her direction. If I managed to get it close to her she would pick it up and carry it off triumphantly. It was my version of throwing a golf ball into the watching crowd after winning a major tournament. Little things please little minds!

The First Cricket Season without Poppi

The Sunday Social team played seventeen games in 2023, and thankfully, as far as Sophie was concerned, she could attend nine of them as they were away from Worcester Park where our canine friends had been banned by cynophobes in 2009. As

I was the captain I attended all seventeen matches, either as a player or as the scorer, which meant that a rather miserable Sophie was left home alone for about seven hours on eight Sundays. As I was in charge of the Midweek team I also had to score for them on five occasions at Worcester Park, which meant that poor Sophie was banned from attending a total of thirteen matches.

Prior to the 2023 season I did not feel too bad about leaving Sophie at home as she had Poppi for company. By the end of the season, however, I decided that the only thing to do was to ditch the captaincy and only make myself available to play in away matches. The decision had been made easier for me when the chairman of the section had accused me of not being 'inclusive', based upon what I considered to be extremely flimsy evidence. After captaining teams at Worcester Park for over fifty years I could not believe what I was hearing. I had been available to play in all the Sunday matches that season but dropped myself on seven occasions so that someone younger could be included. Let's face it that included every other member of the cricket club.

Although Sophie enjoyed meeting several old friends at away games, such as Bill Early at Banstead, who could always be guaranteed to make a fuss of her, her presence seemed to trigger the same response from someone at nearly every game, when they would enquire of me, *"I thought you had two dogs?"* or *"Where's Poppi?"* Having to explain that Poppi had died was still very hard to do, as I still missed her.

Who's a Good Girl, Sophie

In many ways Sophie could be considered to be the perfect dog. She is extremely well behaved, very friendly, cheap to maintain, lets herself into the garden to go to the toilet, is fit and healthy and is the only one of my dogs to have reached the age of ten without being on medication; plus it is interesting to note that she has never ever been physically sick despite eating grass whenever possible.

It was not until after the death of Poppi that Sophie's true character emerged. Unfortunately, and I should really not say this, she does not appear to be very clever, which could be due to her not being a true Border Collie. She is also rather boring as she never gets into any trouble, but there again any dog following in Poppi's footsteps would appear boring.

Sophie tries her hardest to be good but quite often she does not understand simple instructions. When that happens she panics, and either freezes or returns to the safety of her bed. One can ask her to fetch a ball in the house, and although there are plenty lying around, she appears not to understand the question. Occasionally when I am in the kitchen, however, she will produce a tennis ball and drop it behind me. I tap it towards her and she rolls it back, This goes on for about a minute and then she runs away with the ball. Strange game!"

As an ex-Special Needs teacher I can not help but wonder about her apparent lack of intelligence. All my other Border Collies loved playing in the house and were forever running around, either squeaking rubber toys or dropping them in my lap. One could pretend to attack them with a toy rabbit or monkey and they would love to play-fight. Sophie seems, however, to lack this imagination and has never appeared at all interested in playing with any toy, although there are many littering the floor of the living room.

What really amazes me, however, is the fact that she can not recognise my car, although I have owned it for over five years and she has ridden in it hundreds of times. After a round of golf I usually ask her to find the car when we go into the car park. Although my car is a bright blue Kia, some of the cars that she stands excitedly besides, waiting to be let in, look nothing like my car either in shape or colour. Perhaps she just fancies a ride in a large white Discovery.

Probably Sophie's only blemishes in her behaviour were those she picked up from Poppi. She does jerk forward whenever a player is taking a shot on the golf course and when we are crossing a road at a Pedestrian Crossing, although she does not try to attack the box which emits the beeping sound.

Sophie will also bark excitedly whenever she sees a fox, cat, dog or delivery van outside the house. Quite often she will bark just to attract my attention. She then looks at me, whilst wagging her tail, as though she is trying to tell me what she has seen. Unlike Poppi, however, she will stop barking whenever I tell her to, and often replaces the bark with a quiet growl.

Sophie a Very Sociable Animal

Although Sophie will tolerate other dogs she never plays with them. She does, however, love people and will try whenever possible to interact with them by wagging her tail frantically, or by trying to make eye contact, whenever she spots a likely victim. Just a smile from a passing stranger is enough to alert Sophie to the fact that that person is a dog lover and might like to stroke her.

Sophie loves to go shopping with me as it is a great opportunity to meet new people. Although we usually walk into Cheam Village or North Cheam, Sophie really loves it when we take the bus. Sometimes there will be someone to interact with at the bus stop but, if not, she will stand there quietly watching until she sees a bus appear in the distance, when she becomes quite excited and looks at me as though to say, *"The bus is coming."*

Her first reaction when she gets on the bus is to search for food on the floor. My first reaction is to stop her looking for food on the floor. Sophie then looks at the passengers sitting there and tries to make eye contact with as many people as possible. If I see a person smile at her I usually lengthen the lead so that they can stroke her. It is really quite satisfying when one sees the pleasure that some of the elderly passengers obtain from just a few seconds stroking Sophie. It is even more satisfying if that person is in a wheel chair. It is surprising how many strangers talk to me because of Sophie and tell me that they had a Border Collie when they were young.

Sophie knows the shops that we regularly go into and will try to pull me into them, whether I want to go into them or not. She used to love going into the hardware shop as they had open bins full of bird seed at ground level. Sophie also loves visiting the chemist's although her wagging tail does tend to cause havoc to any low level displays.

Once upon a time we used to regularly visit a neighbour called Debbie, and her mother Sheila who suffered from MS and was virtually confined to an armchair. Sophie loved jumping onto Sheila's lap to give her a lick. Fortunately the old lady, who could hardly move, loved it.

It is ironic to record here that my lovely, sweet little dog, Sophie is the only one of my dogs to have put someone into hospital, when she bit Debbie. It was actually Debbie's fault as she left her finger too close to a biscuit that she was giving Sophie, who managed to draw blood. Following a long phone call with 101, Debbie was advised that it might be advisable to get a tetanus injection at A & E, where she spent five hours waiting to be treated.

We have had a few visitors to our home since Poppi died in October 2022, for Sophie to make a fuss of, such as my brother and his daughter Karen, her husband Tony and their two youngest children Louis and Bobbi. They loved |Sophie and she loved them.

Not all of our visitors are dog lovers, however, and poor Sophie still gets the cold shoulder from Sam who always waits outside in the car, with his mother, whilst my nephew Neil takes the brunt of Sophie's welcome. Sam no longer cries and pulls away from her as he used to do ten years ago, however. Now he tends to ignore her

completely whilst she tries to get close to him. The photograph on the left shows Sam sitting on the bench in my garden when he was ten in 2021, with Sophie sitting between Sam's legs. The photograph on the right shows Sam sitting on Sophie's settee last year, with a large coat placed strategically between them.

Apart from Golf days and Cricket matches Sophie and I have not done a lot of socialising since Poppi's death. We do occasionally travel to Ewhurst and visit Carol, Rosemary and Zack and sometimes lunch at one of the lovely rustic pubs in the vicinity, where dogs are welcome, such as 'The Plough' at Oakwood Hill or

'The Scarlet Arms' at Wallis Wood. The photograph on the left shows Carol and Sophie standing in the car park at 'The Parrott' at Forest Green, another marvellous dog-friendly public house.

Sophie loves visiting Carol as she spent a week with her about four years ago when I had a minor operation, as I felt that I could not cope with two dogs. Although Sophie was obviously the easier dog to look after, I did not want to lumber anyone with looking after Poppi because of all her medication. As I always use the speaker on the phone Sophie always knows if I am talking to Carol and usually becomes very excited and jumps on to my lap.

The photograph on the right was one taken by Carol when Sophie stayed with her. It shows her daughter Rebecca and granddaughter Cleo on Holmbury Hill with Sophie and Maya.

Every two or three months Sophie and I tend to meet up for lunch at 'Ye Olde Red Lion' in Cheam Village for a meeting of the Worcester Park Old Farts, which is basically a group of old men who used to play cricket for Worcester Park. Although one or two make a fuss of her, Sophie tends to be ignored by most of them, and spends a couple of hours beneath one of the tables, whilst we all

reminisce about games that we were involved in forty or fifty years ago. In the photograph on the left one can see that her lead is tethered to the base of a table, and behind her is the shoe of one of the Old Farts.

The most enjoyable events for Sophie, since Poppi died, however, were probably the two Christmas parties that we attended at Juliet's farmhouse in 2022 and 2023. Apart from the fact that Juliet has a job, and there are horses in the paddock, her life is very reminiscent of the 1970's sitcom 'The Good Life' in that there are free range chicken strolling around, bee hives and vegetable beds, providing one with eggs, honey and vegetables.

We always eat in a long narrow room which had been a milking parlour many years ago. That was extremely useful this year, as apart from Juliet, her partner Philip, sons Felix and Oscar, there were thirteen guests. To accommodate everyone, three or four tables were placed in a line to form a very long central table which, when covered by various table cloths, was reminiscent of a medieval banqueting hall.

Sophie did have a little spat with Inky, Juliet's tiny dog, but their differences were quickly resolved, and both dogs studiously avoided each other for the remainder of Christmas Day. The photograph on the left shows Inky who was slightly larger than a chicken, but much smaller than Sophie.

Both dogs spent most of the time wandering backwards and forwards beneath the table hoping to snaffle any food which might have been accidentally dropped.

The photograph on the right shows Sophie who had just been caught in the act of standing on her hind legs besides the small table upon which, a couple of hours earlier, there had been a turkey and a goose.

Conclusion

In a way this short book has been an autobiographical account of the last forty two years of my life, in which I have been blessed by having had such great friends and companions as my five Border Collies: Ben, Benji, Gemma, Poppi and finally Sophie. If I had known that I was going to write this book forty two years ago, I would have taken some better photographs.

I hope that you enjoyed reading about my dogs, and found some of the tips useful, although they petered out at number 36. Hopefully you might even think about rescuing a Border Collie from one of the marvellous rescue centres such as the Border Collie Trust GB in Colston, Staffordshire, where I was privileged to meet both Poppi and Sophie, who have added so much to my life.

Although Sophie's understanding of the spoken word is rather limited, she is much more intelligent than I sometimes give her credit for. Lately I have noticed that she has now mastered the art of opening the door between the conservatory and the bed room when it is not securely fastened, plus she never forgets how to perform an activity.

Apart from her hearing, eyesight and sense of smell, which are exceptional, Sophie also appears to be remarkably fit, which I think must be down to her diet of Royal Canin Sensitivity Control, Happy Dog Africa, Burns Chicken and Rice and Youmove tablets, to which I have added Canine Prime in the past year.

Hopefully Sophie will acquire a new companion in 2024, as I am acutely aware that life has been incredibly boring lately, as we have experienced one of the wettest winters on record. The new dog will, of course, be a Border Collie, who hopefully will have the intelligence of Ben; the sensitivity of Benji; the devotion of Gemma; the unpredictability of Poppi and the loving nature of Sophie.